Stand Out!

Lessons for Finding the Leader Within

Fiction by Kenneth Kerns

Stand

Out!

Lessons for Finding the
Leader Within

by Kenneth Kerns

COPYRIGHT INFORMATION

For Shaun and Chanee, and for anyone else with potential that needs help finding the leader within

TABLE OF CONTENTS

INTRODUCTION

When I was a very young kid, I was quiet but sociable, above average but not "gifted," not popular but not ostracized. Every year, I picked seats in the class that were not in the front but not in the back, but always somewhat close to the door. I remember being tested as a sensitive introvert, the early markings already there for a nerd.

Clearly, I did not stand out from the pack.

That began to change fairly quickly.

It is never easy, in retrospect, to find that perfect inflection point in your life where everything changed direction. The truth is, our lives are messy. Every person we meet has an influence on us, a gravitational pull that, like the Moon, can shift the tide when no one is looking.

One of my earliest moments of inflection was in church, when I volunteered to help teach Sunday school. I do not know how or why but soon I grew conflicted with what I was teaching. At the time, I was in fifth grade!

A few years later, inspired by one of my all-time favorite teachers, I wrote my first op-ed piece on how watching television during homeroom was a waste of time.

I should have known then that training would be in my blood.

In high school, as I came out of my shell and went in search of my life's calling, I struggled to stand out in a class full of future doctors, lawyers, computer programmers, and college professors. At the time, I thought I was a bit of a loser for having always been a Secretary, and never the President of the countless clubs I was in. Yeah, sure, I lost elections... a lot of elections... and it sucked, but that is because it never occurred to me to appreciate that I was an officer in quite so many groups.

In college, I was elected to represent my college in Student Government; I founded my own organization to combat student apathy; and supported dozens of candidates and student groups spanning the gamut of causes. I was even treasurer for the Board of College Councils, the largest student-run organization inside Student Government (the only ones that were bigger were the Greek-letter organizations and the one that organized Homecoming).

I never quite caught the brass ring of being elected a club President, no matter how hard I tried. However, I won recognition for my more "behind the scenes" work ethic and was elected by my peers as the Outstanding Student Senator of the semester.

As the intensity of school faded in the rear view mirror, I looked back on those years with a mix of regret and disappointment about what might have been. Despite all I had achieved, I was convinced that I surely had not done enough to stand out among the crowd.

Yet, a curious thing happened to me recently. My workplace instituted a voluntary mentoring program. Some of the employees, all closer to my age, asked me if I would be their mentor. Unfortunately, I was not eligible because the program seeks to match employees with mentors outside of their department. Still, I appreciated being asked, because it was a compliment: ambitious workers now wanted my help in finding success.

This unexpected outcome led me to ask a lot of questions. How did this happen? How did I go from a self-described loser to a well-respected winner, in less than a decade? Also, if I could not help these employees through a program at work, was there some way I could still help them?

In answering those questions, it became clear to me what I should do: write this booklet. In it, I recall the lessons I learned along the way to finding the leader within that I always knew I had but had always struggled to show to other people. I do not pretend that is an ultimate, all-inclusive guidebook, and I do not have the ego to think this would be widely read. However, if there is one thing I have learned as a trainer, it is that if even one person finishes the session with at least one new take away, then you have succeeded.

So, dear reader, I hope you find my perspective to be useful. I also hope it helps you find the leader within, that it inspires you to aspire more, to never give up but be willing to accept a change in your life's calling, and in the end hopefully you will find that ultimate dream job. That is my aspiration for this book. Let us see if I succeed.

Within, you will find 40 lessons I learned, from college life to cubicles to the (not quite) corner office. These lessons are organized into 6 parts, and most are listed in the order I learned them.

The book opens with "Choose Your Own Adventure," a series of lessons about learning to make the most of your early adulthood, by being practical but daring in your choices, and not being afraid to make a change if something is not working for you.

Part two of the book, "The Day Job," covers lessons learned in the real world of earning a paycheck, and all the benefits that come from that. This contrasts with "Shifting Career Goals," which explains how you begin to live beyond the day to day by becoming more ambitious.

"Getting Your Dream Job" is one of the meatier parts of the book, and for good reason. This is a goal we all struggle with, but with a certain amount of luck and a healthy dose of pluck, we can all do it.

To those with leadership in your blood, the part called "Managing a Team" is your part of the book. It will give you tips on how to deal with a very specific role that is not as easy or as glamorous as some people think.

Lastly, "Going Forward" includes a quartet of lessons that are useful for everyone, regardless of where you are along the career track. These four items will serve you well long after you have found the leader within you.

PART ONE: CHOOSE YOUR OWN ADVENTURE

"Everyone is necessarily the hero of his own life story." ~ *John Barth*

Lesson 1: College Matters

Very few of us are child prodigies, Olympic athletes, or fame-obsessed singers. Accordingly, the vast majority of people have no freaking clue who they are or what they want to do with the rest of their lives, never mind have it all figure out when they are teenagers.

Thankfully, there's college.

Now, I know that college is not for everyone, and that with soaring tuition costs and the burden of student loans, obtaining education beyond high school can be a very costly mistake. I know this first hand as, ten years later, I'm still repaying loans from my postgraduate studies.

All the same, I think there is some value to that time of your life, and to attending college. In your late teens and early twenties, very few of us have made any long-term commitments – no spouse, no children, and no mortgage. That gives us freedom to pursue a variety of experiences and to find a world with endless possibilities.

If you are old enough, you may remember the 80s classic book series "Choose Your Own Adventure," where the reader is given a choice at the end of each scene as to what to do next, and the result would take you to a different part of the book, creating multiple different stories out of the same paperback. Young adulthood is like that, full of different possible ways life can turn out, full of potential and possibility.

College is a microcosm for those possibilities. Most of us go to a school away from home. The new location allows us to start fresh, to make new friends and ditch old habits that held us back in high school. The classes come in a variety of interests and levels of difficulty. The people we meet range from the stereotypical to the oddest of oddballs. Our ears will hear languages we have only dreamed about. I would also be remiss if I did not at least remind you of the clichéd experiences that Hollywood likes to exploit: parties, romances, and other kinds of "experiments."

Of course, many of us were not at all interested in those experiences. For us, college was a way station in our chosen careers, one with excellent places to study and check out old books. It also allowed us to dip our toes in other career choices to either affirm our life's direction or make corrections.

So what is the bottom line? Whether you stay for the connections, only show up to tap a keg, or find your life's calling, there is no better place to spend your early adulthood than in the quad or in the library of a college campus.

And for many of us, the road to college required so much work and sacrifice during our teenage years that it only made sense that we try to get the most of the experience.

Meanwhile, employers are increasingly relying on an undergraduate degree as a minimal credential for education. Some of the smartest, most talented folks I've ever met have some college coursework but don't have a degree and find many career doors closed to them. In fact, I know managers with dozens if not hundreds of applicants have tossed out those without degrees – regardless of the rest of the resume – just as a way to winnow the field. Consequently, the closer you are to finishing that degree, the more important it becomes that you actually finish. Otherwise, you are throwing good money after bad.

College matters.

Lesson 2: Picking Your Major Requires a Strategy

Just as with every course in the catalog, not every undergraduate major is created equal. For every all-nighter pulled by the architecture school, there is a keg being tapped by the "rocks for jocks" class. For every neuroscience major interning at the children's hospital, there is a political science student watching Election Night at the local bar.

I have some bad news for you: unless you are busting your ass every night in those tough-as-nails majors, your college degree will probably matter far less than your social connections, innate talent and drive, and your willingness to "pay your dues" by having a crappy first job.

While my first paid job was work-study in college and it turned out to be quite painless, I was also extremely lucky that my first full-time job in a cubicle lead to other career opportunities. Yet, I had a fairly rough six months after graduating. I stretched my credit cards to their limit. I stretched my student loans to their limit. I hesitated to take minimum wage jobs out of fear of never having time to find a better job. Finally, I took a one-week-only campaign job that paid $200 plus expenses.

Many of my classmates were less fortunate. After a frustrating few years, they went into graduate school. Some, after getting a MBA, even enrolled a third time to get their law degree. For many, these degree programs were not related at all to what they studied as undergraduates. Others returned from more exciting locales to live with their parents while trying to get a job at the university in our smallish college town.

Life after college can be tough. These days, with the market saturated with job seekers, even lawyers without an Ivy League degree are likely to struggle after graduating. Whether you have the right credentials or connections, an element of luck will be needed to persevere. Therefore, with the benefit of hindsight, I give you this piece of advice: be practical with your choice of major.

I was a political science major. Part of how I decided was that I liked the subject matter taught in the courses I took. Part of it was that I enjoyed being involved in my college's student government. Frankly, though, a big part of it was because I thought that the major would be easy and many of the other majors I had my eye on either involved retaking a class I did not enjoy in high school (Calculus) or was a major I did not think I needed a degree to pursue.

Journalism, in particular, did not seem to be a very practical choice. One can still be a reporter or a columnist or a photographer on talent alone. Why waste three or four years of tuition on a degree you would not need? And given the way things are going in the newspaper and magazine publishing industry, journalism is hardly a growth industry.

Yet, even political science is not very practical. Volunteering on campaigns will better prepare you for life as a political operative than listening to an academic use statistics to discuss the power of the presidential veto. And based on what I do now, learning organizational development in the business school or even studying adult education would have had been more helpful to me.

However, being practical does not mean everyone should have the same generic major, or that it should solely focus on skills you might want or need on the job. In fact, I cringe every time I hear someone rant against the liberal arts and argue we should cut back to essentials like health, engineering, or business. College has a role beyond just being a funneling and training system for corporate America. Moreover, without knowing with absolute certainty what your career will entail, we should not restrict choice or become too bland in our tastes.

What I mean by practicality is that you need to have a strategy in mind when picking what you study. Your choice of major should allow you to build the kind of skills (or connections) you want to get out of the college experience. Do not use it to cut corners or skip the hard choices. Do not choose to be an art history major because you like looking at nude statues, for example. If you choose art history, choose it because it comes naturally to you and/or it allows you time to explore other interests as well.

For example, consider the double-major. An interesting pairing (for example, Art History and Photojournalism) creates greater value as a set than the two majors would on their own with two separate students.

If I were I to do it over again, I would have been more daring with my choice of major and minor. There are simply too many wannabe political operatives with political science and history on their resumes, and most stumble their way into Law School after that. It was a hardly original or practical choice, and I could have done better.

Please be practical when choosing your major.

Lesson 3: Extra-curricular Activities Matter

Yes, one of the biggest clichés about college is based on a certain amount of truth. College students party a LOT. After all, if you were thrown onto a campus of tens of thousands, would you spend most of your down time back in your dingy off-campus apartment or hauled up in your dorm room, or would you go out and meet people? In this time of your life, when you are surrounded by people your own age, why wouldn't you go to parties?

But for the more introverted among us who dread such social interactions, your next best chance to meet people will come from extra-curricular activities. Yes, I am speaking highly of all those frustrating little distractions we had to suffer through in high school to convince the colleges of our choice that we were deserving of having to pay big bucks for a degree.

If you are an introvert like I was in college, walking up to complete strangers and saying hello can be a terrifying experience. There were many a moment back then where I was required to pass out flyers in the quad and try to convince people to care about an issue. No matter who they were, the point was to reach out to as many people as possible and get them out of their default setting of apathy. I hated every minute of it and found every excuse to help the group in other ways. In my mind, no one wanted to be hassled on their way to class or to work or to their dorm round to crash. Worse, the scripted way of approaching them came off as fake, inauthentic, and possibly disingenuous. And I felt going to parties, unless you were with someone or came with a group, was very much the same sort of thing, in that you had to walk up to strangers and start conversations very randomly.

There was a better way. Clubs, associations, teams, study groups - whatever they are called - these are all opportunities to find other people who share common interests. That common interest is the ice breaker you need to be able to talk to a complete stranger when socializing does not common natural. (As a side note, ice breaker activities are very common in corporate training for exactly this reason, to build a bond before diving into the topic at hand.)

After all, once you volunteer to clean a beach together, you and the complete stranger next to you sure do have at least something to talk about, even if it is just to complain about the sheer volume of garbage our fellow human beings leave in their wake.

The chance to interact with more people during your college years can be quite crucial. There is a reason why fraternities boast of having highly successful people as members – networking matters more to them than almost anything other than who is buying the next keg. In turn, that network helps their members land the good jobs that eventually make them noteworthy as alumni.

This is a crucial time in your life for networking, but I did want to touch on once other reason why clubs are useful. Most college students will undoubtedly focus on finishing their degree, and not so much on landing a job after graduation. Therefore, many graduates will have very thin, almost non-existent resumes. What helps fill in the space on that resume is a list of your extra-curricular activities – and the more variety, the better.

I discovered the importance of extra-curricular activities in a quite random way during my job search after college. As I'll explain in Lesson Six, the search was not going well after several months of burning up my modem emailing resumes. Then, finally, I got a call from the retirement plan organization that would eventually hire me. I found out during the interview that my resume was picked out by the hiring manager at least in part because I had mentioned my very brief stint as a non-voting member on a city pension board.

You could say that my extra-curricular activity was responsible for landing me my first job. It would be a hyperbole, but not all that far from the truth. Sure, I had to pass a test that is notoriously difficult, but I would not have been given a chance if it weren't for the clubs on my resume.

What you do in your spare time during college does matter, both for socializing and networking, but also for making you more marketable in the real world after college. Clubs do matter.

Lesson 4: Find Your Passion

As I said before, young adulthood is about finding yourself and college is a great place to do that. But "finding yourself" is a bit of a cliché for this time in one's life. A more tranquil person might say "finding your bliss." I prefer the term "finding your passion." After all, most people know who they are, for the most part; they just might be at a loss as to what to do with themselves in the real world, for the rest of their life.

As a self-diagnosed introvert, I was never particularly comfortable in social settings at college. All the new people and experiences made it hard to feel comfortable in my own skin. Yet, on many occasions, I found myself in situations where I needed to speak to a group and needed to sound convincing. This never felt like one of my strengths. Fortunately, I received some useful advice one night when several of us were shuttling between club meetings to promote our pet cause. It was originally advice on how to keep my remarks short, but within it I discovered a trick for overcoming self-doubt and self-consciousness: talk only about what you are passionate about, and be passionate about what you talk about.

Years later, Dr. Steven D. Cohen, a communications professor, wrote in his book *Lessons from the Podium* that "when you speak about something that you love, you will feel more at ease and more connected with your audience."

Unfortunately, I did not have that advice at the time. I had to find this out the hard way. I learned it during my time at the University's Student Government.

There are a lot of fun antics I got into as a result of my involvement in campus politics. Some of those antics were inspiration for a series of fiction books I've written, so I won't repeat all of those stories, which included a crowd-sourced filibuster, impeachments, and late nights of watching votes being counted.

Instead, let me just tell you one of the stories from my last year in college. I had been involved in many clubs in my short time there. By my third year, I was treasurer of the Board of College Councils, which was a semi-autonomous organization for the academic groups on campus. I felt very strongly that student groups were often disrespected within Student Government, especially if they did not play the political game the way that the students in charge of approving their budgets had liked. I wanted to be their champion.

Well, after researching how much student groups did versus other things that the Student Government paid for, I decided that the student organizations needed more money. I proposed a budget amendment that would increase the money set aside from student organizations by about $10,000 (an increase of less than 5 percent). This would not take money away from anyone else, despite some well-publicized wasteful spending (including mismanagement in our agencies bringing speakers and musical guests to campus). Instead, the budget increase might require a very small increase in student activity fees.

My amendment was unusual, as the budgets created in committee usually got rubber-stamped by the full Student Senate without much debate. However, the move allowed me to give a speech and was guaranteed to get a vote, so all senators were on record as to whether to give enough money to organizations. My speech was not my best, and the Senate refused after the chairman of the budget committee gave a speech in opposition.

I was not done. The budget vote became an issue fought in dueling editorials in the campus newspaper, and took a prominent role in my pitch for the upcoming elections. My team of lonely underdogs lost those elections, too.

But I had the last laugh. In the spring semester, when the detailed budget for student organizations was being finalized, the budget committee began realizing the value in what these student organizations did for the campus. They decided to propose their own budget amendment, which was virtually identical to the one I had proposed not six months earlier. They acknowledged that I was in the right, so I tried to not rub it in too much. That success probably made it easy to accept that my tenure in Student Government was reaching an end.

Years later, when Dr. Cohen was asked about our shared history in college, and people asked about the kind of person I was then, he was nice enough not to tell any embarrassing stories, but did tell my coworkers that I was passionate. Mission accomplished.

Lesson 5: Know When It's Time to Move On

As I said, it is fully expected that not all who start college will ever finish it. Even among the more studious of people, there are also plenty of us who may have the talent but not the drive to finish. On the other hand, for every person who stops at the right moment, there are also some who do not know when to quit and, like an addict, find themselves taking on more than they can handle. It happens. You just have to know your limits, recognize a burn out moment, and respond by moving on.

In the fall of my third year of college, 9/11 happened. A month later, my mother had a stroke at a young age; she survived but had to quit working. That same semester, I managed a failed Student Government political party and was taking a 5-credit crash course in Portuguese.

I too survived that semester, and found myself 3 credits short of graduating. That spring, I took it relatively easy – an independent study, an online class, and two other classes. Since I was guaranteed of graduating early, I applied to several graduate schools. My first acceptance was from UF's political campaigning program, giving me an option to stay in Gainesville for two more years. Using that option, I campaigned hard to be President of UF's Board of College Councils, a job I really wanted and felt I worked hard to earn, but I did not get it. My independent study did not go that well and my other extra-curricular activities proved more frustrating than usual that spring semester.

In early April, I was accepted into the graduate school of political management (GSPM) program at George Washington University. Just as my semester was winding down, I had a decision to make – stay with the frustrating but familiar comfort of my hometown, or make a drastic change by moving 800 miles north to D.C.

All of my friends and closer acquaintances expected me to stay in Gainesville. But I remembered a conversation I had weeks earlier. Glenda Frederick, a professional I knew, stunned me with the blunt assessment that "you look ready to move on, if you ask me." She had noticed that I had run out of ideas for fixing Student Government in small and easy ways. I had also run out of options in my extra-curricular activities, especially since I steered clear of the fraternities and of the University's leadership honoraries. She might not have known everything, but she knew like I did that I had a trying year and my academic record was slipping a bit.

I had reached my limit and needed a change. So, to DC I moved. It was a good thing, too. If it weren't for the GSPM option, I might not have had the career that would lead to this book.

So the lesson learned was quite simple: Do not stay put in a situation that is not doing you or others any good. Sometimes moving on is the only option, no matter how scary, unpredictable, or uncertain the future may be.

PART TWO: YOUR DAY JOB

"The best way to appreciate your job is to imagine yourself without one." ~ Oscar Wilde

Lesson 6: A Job is a Start

When you are first starting out, it can be tough to find a job in your particular field. Metrics that made you a stand out in school no longer matter much. Grade point averages, SAT scores, club presidencies - none of these things matter much, if at all, to an employer. Heck, unless you are in a highly technical field, even your college major matters very little. Instead, your degree proves you can be trained and would have the self-discipline to stick with a project until the end. Maybe, just maybe, some of those other thin lines on your resume will help show what kind of person you are and what skills you possess, so they are not without any value, just not enough to keep on your resume for too long.

A number of employers either have low expectations for entry-level positions or have an on-boarding program for bringing new hires up to speed. A few even have both. This helps the organization remain realistic but it can be a very disheartening experience for a young, ready-to-take-on-the-world idealist.

When I moved to DC for graduate school, it was literally a week after I turned 21. After a few days of sight-seeing, and in between classes at GW, I spent the next several months looking for a full-time position that would get my foot in the door on Capitol Hill, in campaigns, or just in government in general. I was determined to make use of my new college degree in political science. With luck, I was interviewed in my first week for a job at the Government Accountability Office (GAO). The interview itself was rather short, but we spent a lot of time checking out the workspace, meeting potential coworkers. Then, they set me down in an empty cubicle to complete a couple tests. I spent the better part of an entire day at the GAO. Unfortunately, I did not get it.

My job search did not go well after that. Two months of applications and emails, I was getting desperate. The only other potential opportunity I had was on Capitol Hill for a congresswoman who lost her re-election a few weeks later, shutting the door on that chance. So, I took a break from D.C. to go work in New Jersey for the final week of the late Senator Lautenberg's re-election campaign.

Being a paid volunteer on a campaign was interesting. I did it again two years later in North Carolina. The Lautenberg operation was a bit more disorganized, due in no small part to the fact that Lautenberg was a last-minute candidate to replace the original nominee. During that week, I met a number of people my own age, and got my first real shot at "networking" beyond getting to know my classmates and teachers at GW.

As I came home from New Jersey, I checked the answering machine for messages and found one worth keeping. Joan Poindexter, a manager at the UMWA Health and Retirement Funds, wanted me to call her back to set up an interview for a pension processing position. The Funds interview was very similar to the GAO process, except that most of the discussion took place after the test, not before. They gave me a multiple-choice test and an essay-writing test. In both they gave me at least double the amount of time I needed, which surprised Joan. Later, in talking with her I made a nervous gaffe where I mistook the Washington Redskins for the FSU Seminoles (although they have admittedly similar team colors and logos). Yet, the interview went well. She asked me about my resume, including a couple items that were most relevant to the work of The Funds.

Maybe a week later, I had a job offer. Even though the job was in retiree benefits and not in politics, I took it. Not only was the pay, hours, and benefits better than anything I could have hoped to get in an entry-level position answering phones on Capitol Hill, but the job itself was a nice challenge. It helped me get out from under my mounting debt and I thought it would give me the time to look for that elusive political job and might even help me get it.

Indeed, shortly after finishing me degree, I got another interview on Capitol Hill, with a Senator representing West Virginia, a state that has a lot of UMWA retirees that I worked with. That interview turned out to be entry-level, a front-desk receptionist job and I just knew it was not going to be a good fit.

Still, I learned a valuable lesson. A job is a job, and sometimes it is more important to get any job to help pay the bills than to satisfy one's career ambitions.

A job is a start, a foot in the door. It is what you do with that opportunity that will determine if you go places.

Lesson 7: Pensions Are Important

In my early twenties, when most of my high school classmates were still trying to finish college and find their life's calling, I was already in my first "real" job. I was helping the Baby Boomer population sign up for the retirement benefits they earned over a lifetime of working in difficult jobs such as construction, trucking, and most especially coal mining.

Most people in their twenties are very short-term focused: their dates on Friday night, what clubs they'll hang out at on Saturday, how they're going to spend their next paycheck on the latest iPhone. I was like that, too. I arranged my work schedule to be convenient for my studies. I took vacations to see my brother's high school graduation in Florida or to visit my father for Thanksgiving regardless of the cost of plane tickets.

When I was first hired, a manager in Human Resources spent an hour with me filling out paperwork and signing me up for various employee benefits. Then, she put the 401(k) enrollment form in front of me. I had a vague idea of what a 401(k) was; that it was something older Americans depended on in addition to Social Security. But I did not know what were the right questions to ask about it. The best I could come up with was repeating something I had heard before.

"Can I roll this over when I leave?" I asked.

She said yes, and without knowing anything else to ask, I signed up for the bare minimum just so I wouldn't have to remember later.

As I became more familiar with pension plans, I got to understand the right questions to ask. I increased my contributions so that I would take full advantage of the employer match. I examined the investment options and tweaked them to match my more risk-averse nature.

Then, I asked how this program differed from a pension. It turns out that this was a very important question. 401(k) savings accounts, even though they are rapidly replacing older employer-paid retirement programs, are not like the typical pensions of yore. I was fortunate that my employer had two different programs, and after 5 years I would be vested under the second program.

Pensions come in two forms: defined benefit and defined contribution. Recent innovations, called hybrid plans, combine the most popular elements of both.

Defined benefit (DB) plans quite literally define the benefit that is intended to be paid, usually in the form of a monthly annuity that reflects service and salary. The employer bears the costs and risks associated with funding that plan. Most of the older retirement programs are DB in nature, and are what most of us think of when we hear the word "pension." The organization for which I work administers a DB plan for the nation's coal miners.

Defined contribution (DC) plans, on the other hand, shift most of the funding and all of the risk to the individual participant. Individuals have more responsibility under DC plans to understand how to invest for the future. It is possible that DC plans can earn a higher benefit, but the individual, not the employer, risks losing some or all of the account value in a bad investment. 401(k) plans, IRA accounts, and employee stock purchase plans are the most popular forms of DC plans. These plans are generally cheaper for the employer and easier for the employee to take with them to a new job (through "portability" or "rollover" provisions).

There are nuances and details about pensions that I could spend a lot of time discussing, but building one's retirement plan is not the point of this book or this lesson.

At this point, I was hired into an organization that provided retirement benefits to thousands, to do a job involved in enrolling future beneficiaries into those benefits. Whether I was age twenty or age fifty, given the nature of my work and of my employer, it should have been obvious to me that knowing my own benefits would be important.

Being knowledgeable of my own benefits would help me answer questions of the applicants I would be working with. Not because the details are the same (because they weren't). Instead, it would help because I could better understand where confusion would come up and could anticipate what details the applicant would want to know but about which they could not even think of asking.

You can broaden this lesson out a bit. A realtor who herself only rents apartments may not be as prepared as they could be to help wannabe homeowners. A Hollywood writer who never watches movies or television may never be able to understand why none of his projects succeed.

Basically, I found that the skills you learn on the job can help you in your private life, and that your own private experiences inform your approach to your day job. Most of us will find success if we resist the temptation to fully compartmentalize our work and private worlds.

Lesson 8: The Benefits of Benefits

Okay, so not every workplace has pension benefits these days. Some employers even see the offering of a 401(k) type of retirement benefit as a luxury that they do not need. Yet, most companies provide benefits of some sort. After all, a salary is not the only way to attract and retain talented workers.

The exact type of benefits will vary from company to company. In larger organizations with different divisions and field offices, it's possible that the benefits will vary even within a company.

The biggest and most important are the medical, dental, and vision insurance benefits. How much do you have to pay in premiums? What is the deductive? Co-pay? What is covered? Does the company participate in the Flexible Spending Accounts and related systems that help defray the employee cost with pre-tax dollars?

Other benefits might include flexible scheduling, telecommuting, paid vacation, and paid sick. Seniority might also matter, especially in union shops, with longevity granting pay increases or first-dibs on promotions.

Early in my career, the only benefit I truly cared about was tuition reimbursement. The IRS currently allows the first $5,200 per year in tuition reimbursements to be excluded from compensation (meaning that it is tax-free). The IRS's dollar limit on the tax write-off is often used as the limit a company would provide in tuition reimbursement; anything above that would be considered taxable compensation, so there is less interest in exceeding that amount.

When I was first hired, I had a pile of debt on credit cards due to not working for an extended period of time. The student loans I was adding to that pile were barely covering tuition at the graduate program I was attending at GW. I figured I could use $5000 in free money to help sort out my cash flow issues.

So what was the catch? I needed to get pre-approved to take the coursework, pass the classes, and still be with the Funds at the end of the semester.

The pre-approval was easy since the classes were part of a degree program and having a master's degree could open promotional opportunities I might not otherwise be able to get. Passing the classes took work, but was never in doubt. So the real tough part was avoiding the temptation to hunt for my next job while waiting for the reimbursement check.

I did this in each spring semester of 2003 and 2004. Pursuing a master's degree thus gave me $10,000 in benefits – which was better than five months' worth of take-home pay – above and beyond my salary, helping me when I needed it most.

Needless to say, the benefit of using your benefits can be easy to quantify. Not everyone is in a position to go back and finish college or start a graduate degree. You might have young kids at home, or you might be caring for a sick relative. So, tuition reimbursement may not be for everyone, but having the benefit available can certainly help you decide whether to continue your studies. Even without tuition, chances are that your employer has a benefit you can take advantage of, that is perfect for you at this point of time.

You would be silly not to take advantage of the benefits you are entitled to while you still can.

Lesson 9: Skills Are Transferable

This seems like an easy lesson. After all, learning to photocopy notes for a class is the same as learning to photocopy reports for the boss. Obviously, the lesson I learned here was more subtle than that.

In my first year at work, people at work knew I was going to graduate school and that I had been a bit of A political and legal nerd. This led them to even nudging me to take the LSAT to see if I could get into Law School. I was too debt-conscious and concerned what my potential score might mean, so I declined. (By the way, given recent reports of former law students that are heavily in debt and finding it difficult to find legal jobs, I probably dodged a financial bullet by ignoring my coworkers' advice.)

My legal nerd status stemmed in part from my service on the Grievance Committee of the small and independent employees' union that organized my work place. It probably also didn't hurt that I actually liked reading the Plan documents of our Pension Plan. Another reason what that I had mentioned that during my time in Student Government I had earned a nickname – the "walking Constitution" – for my ability to cite rules from the top of my head. However, it was not until the recall of a Union President that my legal nerd credentials were firmly entrenched.

This Union President had a larger-than-life personality for an organization filled with analytical, introverted folks. She was quite frank with her opinions, which lead to many disagreements. One of the more high-profile rivalries she had was with a co-worker in her same work unit. They competed to get their work done, competed for recognition from Management, and would often take opposite sides in disputes about the work they reviewed of their other co-workers.

One day, her rival needed her help in her capacity as Union President. She refused. I do not remember the exact details of their dispute today, but needless to say her rival did not appreciate the lack of support. By then, this President had made a few too many enemies within the Union, and her rival had many friends in the field offices. The rival's friends felt the President had gone too far in letting her personal opinions shape her official actions.

They decided to take an unprecedented step of attempting a recall, which required gathering signatures on a petition alleging misuse, abuse, or neglect of office. Those friends were not popular with the staff as a whole, so for political reasons they did not want to be seen leading the charge on recall and impeachment.

Even though I had no strong feelings about the ordeal, they recruited me to be their spokesman. The Union bylaws specified that what would happen next is the appointment of a neutral "judge." An official hearing then would be held to determine the specificity and validity of the charges.

I read through the bylaws, made sure I understood the complaints people had with the President, and prepared a detailed argument of how her actions went against the requirements set in our bylaws.

During the hearing, I played the part of prosecutor well enough. The President had not expected the need to put up much of a defense, so she had very little to say in response. After some deliberation, the impeachment judge reluctantly agreed with the case I laid out after noting with dismay the lack of any defense.

The Union President was thus recalled and removed from office. After a reshuffling of officers, I was brought into the Union Executive Board as Grievance Chair, a position I held for seven years.

If I hadn't built up my legal skills through Student Government, I probably would not have been able to make the case against that President, and would not have been given a voice in leading the Union.

In an unrelated case of transferring skills, my penchant for writing fiction has helped me become a natural choice for writing most of my office's training materials even though I'm not the training manager.

The lesson I learned was that even if the reasons for learning a skill are silly or immature, you may never know how or when it will be useful to have that skill in your back pocket.

Lesson 10: Management is Not Perfect

Thanks in small part to lampooning in the Dilbert comic strip, this lesson is pretty engrained in the American psyche, so you might be surprised to see me include it here.

Yet, the reality is that most of us carry a generic sense of respect for the authority of Management, and find our ambitions steered toward joining their elite ranks. For the inexperienced, that could result in giving those in Management too much credit for the ingenuity and pure luck that comes from their decision-making.

I found out fairly early on that not everyone in Management has the Midas touch. In fact, often times, they are in over the heads and could be acting on less than accurate information. The earliest example of these was when

I was given an "oral reprimand" for tone in a letter to a beneficiary.

First, the irony of oral reprimands at my workplace was that these were not just formal parts of a disciplinary system, but that as such they had to be written down. So my "oral" warning was not oral at all.

Secondly, tone is often subjective, especially in the written word. Sarcasm, for example, is harder to get across in email or text than in face-to-face conversations. It can also be influenced by the reader's mindset at the time of the reading. If you're having a bad day, or think the author is out to get you, you will have a vastly different response to the same email than if you were happy and were chatting with your best friend. Tone, thus, is very hard to define and near impossible to prove to a third-party. Too often, it gets reduced to a "I'll know it when I see it" kind of definition.

Thirdly, this discipline occurred six months after the letter was written, and was oddly timed around other events happening at the workplace that convinced me, whether true or not, that part of this ordeal over misinterpreted tone was retaliatory.

So what was the offending tone? I'm paraphrasing now, since this incident took place a decade ago, but it was something to the effect of, "You've applied on this date, this date, and that date, and again today. You have not submitted new information so we've denied you again. You will remain denied until you submit information that will change the outcome."

The applicant was, at this point, had been applying every few years in the vain hope that a new person would give him a different result. The applicant might not have known this, but we keep records of every prior decision and would not change anything unless we discovered a mistake or received new information.

Yes, I was matter-of-fact about his situation; some might say blunt. Yet, our form letters for such denials use nearly identical language.

So, when this came up in my meeting with HR, I asked where my tone went wrong, or how they would say it differently. The response was a blank stare, a repeated assertion that the tone was obviously wrong and them asking why I couldn't see that. I asked if they had other examples, noting I wrote literally dozens of letters a day in the six months since, and they said they had none, only that "this one came to our attention just recently."

There are some fundamental things they teach you in Management School. (And as corny as that sounds, there are organizations dedicated to providing training for new managers, and I attended several such seminars when I became a manager and a supervisor.) The first is there should be no surprises in performance reviews or discipline sessions. The second, feedback should be timely. Thirdly, feedback should be specific. Lastly, if an employee needs to correct behavior, actual suggestions should be brought forward so the appropriate expectations are set.

This situation basically failed all of those points. Having only one letter out of thousands – an old one at that – where the tone was unacceptable came as a surprise; this was certainly not timely; and the whole ordeal made a mountain out of an ant's footprint on a molehill. Their feedback was vague and non-specific, and thus they had no concrete suggestions for changing the letter or how to be more careful in the future.

The discipline was a complete and utter failure. At the time, I latched onto the retaliatory angle, but in hindsight, I think they were being put through that meeting because Management felt like they had to do something only because that applicant had complained.

If I were handling this now, from the other side of the table, I would not have let this get to the point of a meeting with HR. I am not even sure I'd ever bring up "tone" as an issue unless it was within a documented pattern of behavior. But even as part of a pattern, I would have informally talked to the employee before it got anywhere, and when I did I would give specific feedback on what went wrong and how to fix it.

So I learned early on that Management is not perfect. I have since learned from other experiences that not everyone in Management should be a manager, nor should it be everyone's ambition to join those ranks. You have to know how to handle performance issues and you have to know how to handle potentially tough conversations. That said, if you are on the receiving end of one of Management's talks, you have to remain calm and listen to their side. Most of the time they make sense and they have valid points to make. You just have to know that you can and should defend yourself if they are wrong.

Your Manager has authority, but may not have credibility. Credibility is earned, not had by default. It's a lesson that I have returned to repeatedly in recent years as I transitioned into my dream job and beyond.

Lesson 11: Be Concise

It may seem ironic that a self-help book which takes several pages to explain each and every pithily titled lesson would include a lesson like this, yet I assure that it most definitely makes sense.

A lot of us find ourselves getting long-winded when we communicate. Sometimes we are talkative with our friends. Other times, we are writing 10,000 word essays on why our jobs are giving us carpal tunnel.

And if you are the shy or introverted type, you might have landed in a job that requires a lot of solitary, analytical work that you then have to write up to give to someone higher up in the corporate food chain.

I learned the hard way that, when it comes to the written word in the workplace, shorter is better.

Consider the following example. It happened to me just this morning while I was writing an email to a friend. I was going to send this:

"She sent it to me using this screenwriting software, Final Draft, which we both happen to have and like."

I realized that was wordy and the friend did not need to read the extra verbiage and detail, so I edited it down to this:

"She sent it to me using screenwriting software we both have."

There was no good reason I couldn't send her the original version, since this was a friendly chitchat about non-work matters. However, if I wanted to send something to my boss, should I give him details he doesn't care about, or should I just get to the point? Well, as I'll explain in a later lesson, most bosses do not have the time or personality to care about details all that much, so brevity in work emails is important. Of course, you have to relay the important information, but you don't have to waste his time – or yours – typing up the extra credit stuff.

Brevity is a sought-after quality in aspiring workers because most bosses would like to think of themselves as having that quality. Even the best writer at the company, with great literary flourishes to their prose, is not going to impress the guys upstairs if time is being wasted reading through unnecessary extras.

In fact, there are times when those extra words can land you into trouble.

After I was "kicked upstairs" to quality control work, part of my job entailed reviewing the work of my former peers, critique their work product, and correct it if I can. Sometimes I would get irritated either at a repetitious error or at an individual who would compile more errors than anyone else. That began seeping into my everyday write-up of errors, even to the point where I used the same blunt language regardless of whether I felt the irritation.

The person on the receiving end of the communication could tell my tone, entirely because of a few, unnecessary extra-credit words I could have left out. For example:

"The processor again failed to award credit for time worked in 1975. They did not bother to order a wage record or ask for proof of time worked."

Pretty bad, huh? "Again." "Failed." "Did not bother." There is nothing wrong with being matter-of-fact in your writing, especially in critiquing work. But here, the extra words conveyed a tone that distracted from the message.

Let's try that example again with more brevity:

"Credit for 1975 should have been pursued."

This revised critique is much cleaner, faster to type, and devoid of words and tone that are open to interpretation. Now, if I had a genuine concern about a coworker forgetting a key step in their work, I could raise it with them or their manager in person and "offline" from the official review process.

There is a time and a place for your style and personality to shine through, even in how you convey your message. However, you also have to learn to rein in that part of yourself when attempting to write in a professional manner for a diverse audience. If you can do that, you are well on your way to finding and landing your dream job.

Lesson 12: Find a Hobby

Between sleep, getting dressed, traveling, and actually doing work, for 260 days out of the year, most of our time is consumed by work. However, the weeknights, weekends, holidays, and time off are ours to do with as we please. That is, unless you are lucky enough to have a loved one and a family back home.

For many of us, naps and reading will be great fillers of that time. That cannot be all of it. So, periodically I like to remind myself of this particular lesson: extra-curricular activities matter.

Even as a working adult, clubs and activities are useful, and I am not just talking about ways to fill your free time on the weekends.

First, consider hobbies as a form of stress release. This is obviously true for sports like boxing, but even a quiet activity like writing can be cathartic. As long as you are doing something you love, it can balance out the frustrations of your day job.

I would personally recommend finding hobbies that stand in strong contrast to your work. If you are in a number-crunching job, find a creative outlet. If you find your mind numbed out by work, then engage the physical through the gym or sports.

Whatever you choose, having a hobby is important. You cannot be solely defined at work by what you do at work, lest you become labeled as a workaholic. That is not necessarily a bad thing, as workaholics that do well in their jobs are trusted to do more. However, being seen as a workaholic can actually be a detriment if you want to move beyond that first job. For example, it humanizes you when coworkers discover that other dimension about you that shows you have outside interests. The bosses will also begin to think of you as a better-rounded person that is capable of handling more and different responsibilities if you have hobbies that exercise skills that stand in contrast with your work.

So get out there and find something interesting to do when you are not at work.

Lesson 13: Know When to Look for Promotions

The youngest generation at work is always more prone to job-hopping than any other age group. My fellow Millenials, though, may have taken it to a whole new level. At least until the Great Recession, the knock on Millenials was that (generally) they would never stay in a job for more than six months, and certainly not more than 2 years.

Why? The youngest workers are actively searching for that elusive Dream Job.

Before finding a spouse, starting a family, paying for the house and college tuition, most young Americans are merely looking for their life's calling, a Dream Job to keep them animated about coming to work for more days in the year than we had ever gone to school.

For many of us, that journey is just not that easy. Maybe we are having hard time figuring out what we want out of life. Maybe we have obstacles in front of us preventing us from taking that next step.

One thing we can do is look out for opportunities for change or advancement at the day job. That is what I did about two years after starting my day job. I had gotten comfortable with the work, and had realized I was no longer learning anything new from it. Just as I was getting the itch to leave so that I could make better use of my new graduate degree, an opportunity came up. It would be a promotion to processing benefit claims that involved an ex-spouse's court order for a portion of a pension. The position required a little more flexibility in applying the rules in a slightly different way in each case, and would involve a bit more unpredictability in the kind of work each day would bring. It was just what I needed to stick around at the company for a little while longer. As it turns out, if I had quit my job to change careers rather than take the promotion, I would be in a very different place professionally, and there's no guarantee it would be nearly as good as I have it now.

Take it from me. It may turn out that your dream job is just one promotion away, and you just don't know it yet. Pass up one opportunity, and you may never find it ever again.

Part Three: Shifting Career Goals

"Being ready isn't enough; you have to be prepared for a promotion or any other significant change." ~ Pat Riley

Lesson 14: Change Is Not Always In Your Control

A career often takes unexpected turns; you cannot always expect to have control over where you end up. That is part of the fun of it, but it is also not a lesson that can be easily learned.

Even as I was first getting promoted, I had heard about a reorganization in my department that might create additional opportunities for advancement. I did not really expect much to come of it, however. The organization I work for operates with an employees' union, such that many promotions are dictated solely by seniority. As a young and a recently hired employee, I would be near the bottom of the list of applicants for any new positions; I just got lucky with the Special Payments Analyst position that the job was too complicated and so full of legalese that pretty much no else wanted it.

My luck was surely not going to help me land the new Coordinator role that Management was developing. After all, the four seats for this position were intended to supplant four existing positions in our quality control unit. Each of the four incumbents would likely have first crack at the position, and then anyone else at the Funds who passed all the tests and had been with the company longer would be offered the job. Despite the low odds, I applied.

Yet, my luck won out. Due to the fluke results of some tests, I actually ended up being the second in line for a Coordinator spot. Management asked me if I wanted it, and I told them I would think it over. After all, I had only just got promoted seven months prior, and was finally seeing my workload slow down to a sustainable level. Was I ready to give up a job I knew in favor of one I didn't? I was not sure.

A week went by, and then another. There was no follow-up from Management, and I completely forgot about it, as I got swept up in my work and in the Thanksgiving holidays.

Then, I got a notice from Human Resources that my promoted would be started effectively yesterday. Ready or not, intentionally or not, I was being kicked up stairs.

I was not the only one affected by the reorganization. Several people found themselves laid-off, and others were shuffled into roles that were new and largely undefined and out of jobs to which they were accustomed. We even ended up with a training specialist who was not particularly interested in doing training, but liked the coordinator role even less.

This is a long way of saying that a change in your career is not always in your control. Sometimes, your employer will reorganize, reduce its workforce, or terminate your employment. While we all would prefer to have control over our destiny, that's not always possible. It is far better to learn how to deal with change and its consequences than to think you can dictate what is going to happen to you.

Just remember, everything happens for a reason. The love of your life, the dream job, and the corner office… any of these things could be just around the corner, if you are patient.

Lesson 15: Be the Best at Your Job

While you are biding your time for the next great opportunity, you will face a choice at your day job. Will you do the minimum to avoid getting fired, will you be an average performer who is easily forgotten, or will you do everything to stand out?

I stacked the deck with those choices, didn't I? Of course. Yet, that is essentially the choice you are given with any particular job you intend to keep.

You might not want to draw attention to yourself, especially if your office is large and/or filled with loud and outsized personalities. So your natural inclination may be to do little more than the minimum or average work. That is a perfectly acceptable way to go, especially when you are new to a position or find yourself in a job you really do not like. In fact, being average can subvert any low expectations your boss may already have for your performance.

But... I want you to know that it okay to be good at your job. Heck, there is absolutely nothing wrong with being the best at your job.

Some of the larger companies are recognizing that not everyone wants to be in management even as everyone wants some semblance of a career. That is how companies can end up with people in positions like "Creative Director" or "Technical Director" where one's expertise and value is recognized without requiring them to also deal with leading a team. Maybe that is a viable route you can take in your field. Daniel Tobin, among others, has written extensively on the different career paths and has valuable advice to give on that subject. I myself will get to your dream job in a later lesson.

If a technical career path is one you want to take, then becoming the best in your current job is just about the best way possible to get recognized and then promoted. Yet, even if your interest lies in joining the ranks of management, being good at your current job will not steer you wrong. Contrary to popular belief, most well-run companies will not promote you on seniority or popularity alone. Also, most companies, especially the smaller ones, still believe in management being the most logical place to promote their star performers. After all, if you are good at your job, maybe you can coach others into doing as well as you did.

But what if you do not want to get promoted, at least not at this current job? Good character references from a former boss can go a long way toward you getting hired at your next job. You should not want a dream job to be lost because you were mediocre at your last job.

Now, don't fret if you simply can't compete against the best of your co-workers. Not everyone has the talent (or patience) to be the one to wreck the curve for everyone else. Yet, staff members who are seen as most improved or are least are consistent and reliable can be just as valuable. Sometimes, just having the ambition to try to compete will do you and your career wonders.

Lesson 16: Pick Your Battles Wisely

When we are little, we are told about the little boy who cried wolf. It is a fairy tale told to frighten children about the consequences of lying, particularly repetitive lying.

An extension of that lesson is the importance of being careful about when and how often you raise issues. If you are always bad-mouthing your coworkers' performance because they do not measure up to your standards, no one is going to listen to you when you discover a more legitimate issue that needs to be addressed.

For example, our training specialist had a reputation for not liking how we operated. It was thought that she believed most of us were incompetent and should be fired, even those of us who were the best in the department (and arguably better than she was). It is not clear just how much she had earned that reputation, but as with the boy who cried wolf, that hardly mattered.

When an employee proved incapable of mastering his new job and she told the manager that he was not ready, the manager did not believe her. The manager assumed it was just run-of-the-mill negativity from her. We only found out later just how right she was, and we ended up letting that employee go after having to fix dozens of his mistakes.

Senior management types are generally busy folks. They have board members, government officials, stakeholders, among others, to which they are answerable. They have managers reporting to them, who have staff underneath them. They have projects to manage, crises to handle, and deadlines to meet. When working at that high level, these people just do not have time for every little issue that comes up. Time management is an acquired skill for those at the very top.

That is why you need to be selective in what you raise and when you raise it with them. The less frequent you come to them with a problem, the more likely they will listen and treat it as serious.

I learned this lesson in fall 2008. I jokingly referred to the lesson as being "good things come when you scream." I obviously do not mean that, so let me explain.

The department I worked in had several teams doing similar tasks, and each team was given a morale budget to spend on lunches, recognition items, and other trinkets. Each team had a different manager, and each manager had a different way of interacting with their team. Some team members were able to telework part of the time, and others did not.

By fall 2008, one of the managers had begun to suspect that an employee who teleworked was spending too much time goofing off while at home. She began scrutinizing the employee to the point that it aggravated the person. The employee went to the president of the employees' union, and they in turn came to me as grievance chair almost every day with a new complaint. These complaints were usually anecdotes about how the manager would overreact and overgeneralize about one-time problems. None of the complaints were sufficient to file a grievance, as our contract forbids any grievances over the right to telework, and I told them this.

Of course, my response to the issue was not popular with the union, and as I heard more complaints, I got frustrated that the situation wasn't getting any better.

I do not remember exactly what the trigger was, but during a meeting between coordinators and managers, I made it plainly known that everyone knew about the difficulties, and that it was having a corrosive effect on morale. I also mentioned other festering issues, such as how one team was using their morale budget for movie tickets and the others were not using theirs much at all. I was very forceful in my tone, suggesting that the problems had reached a point where they could not be ignored any longer – especially the ones affecting the frustrated teleworker.

During that meeting, the coordinators and I suggested that the managers address the other issues we raised but we proposed creating a single program for recognizing and rewarding performance achievements. (I'll talk more about that program in the next lesson.)

If I had gone to the managers with every anecdote at the time I had heard them, or raised my voice any time I got angry, I know it would have a "boy who cried wolf" kind of effect on them. I know this because, years later, when one of the managers allowed their emotions to determine their tone, it had just that effect. Fortunately, because I was the messenger for other people's issues rather than my own, and because I rarely spoke out in a decisive manner, I believe that choosing to speak out on that particular day got my supervisors to sit up and take notice of how serious the issues had become.

Later, I would hear from the managers that my efforts in late 2008 and early 2009 were an opportunity to develop and display leadership skills, and that I was successful in seizing that opportunity, all because I was careful in deciding when and what to fight for.

Now, I cannot guarantee it will always work. You are bound to lose some of the battles you fight. However, if you time them properly, you have a better chance at winning. And winning one battle gets you closer to winning the next one.

Lesson 17: Change Is Not Easy

Just as change is not always in your control, most people do not react well to change. Sometimes it helps to imagine how difficult it must be to be the one delivering that change, knowing how people might react.

I learned this lesson the hard way in 2009, when my fellow coordinators and I proposed a change to the way we used our team budgets. Then, my coworkers insisted that I be the public face of the program.

First, some background. For several years, our department had been tracking performance by counting the number of cases approved or denied by our processing and quality review staff. We had set a specific goal for each position based on past performance, and then pro-rated the expectation for each month based on the actual hours worked. Over time, we added other measures for error rates, returning calls, and following up on correspondence.

Each team had also received a morale budget for lunches, birthday cakes, and other forms of recognition. My team devised a way to focus our budget and recognition on achievements in performance. We offered them movie tickets in exchange for a combination of scores that exceeded expectations, kind of like the raffle tickets you would win in an arcade.

Well, after several issues came to a head at the end of 2008, it was agreed that all of the teams should have a similar program. That initially seemed quite easy. After all, each of our processing teams did similar work, had a similar budget, and everyone wanted to participate.

Then things got interesting. Our managers wanted to ensure other teams in the department were able to join in the fun, and they wanted us to structure the rewards so that each person had measurable goals and have a reasonably equitable chance at winning tickets.

This change required us to find ways to measure positions which previously had no obvious goals, much less ones that could be measured by accessing a database query. It also required some creativity to ensure each person could theoretically earn up to 15 points in any given month while giving appropriate weight to the more important pieces of everyone's job.

Once we could do all that, we had to present the plan in a big meeting. The presentation had to be done in such a way that everyone affected could be convinced to take part in this new incentive program.

Now, understand that our workplace is chock full of introverts, even among those in positions of authority. Each of the other coordinators at the time had an intense fear of public speaking and was not as comfortable with all of the math that our plan would require, whereas I was the one who had defined the formulae for our group and had been giving speeches in public since high school. (That fact probably should have been my first clue that my self-identification as an introvert was probably incorrect.)

All the same, this would be my first public speech pretty much since I left grad school almost five years prior. It was also my first speech involving a prop; in this case, a PowerPoint presentation. Never mind that this would have some pretty high stakes, since management was letting us roll out the program and be in charge of it.

How did we do?

Well, managing change is not that different from managing issues, and I happened to have a degree in the doing the latter. The principles of issues management include identifying the components of each issue, identifying potential obstacles and potential allies, and putting together a coalition, all as preemptive measures before an issue becomes untenable.

In some ways, the managers' frustrating efforts to bring conformity to our program actually helped us follow those principles. As maddening as it was to find ways to measure the previously immeasurable for several of our more clerical staff, the ability to present a plan that included them on the same level as the others made it easier for them to support the plan.

Of course, even after the speech, there were bumps in the road. As I said, our staff is mostly introverted, so concerns were left unsaid at the presentation that had to be fixed later. Also, some of the self-reporting needed to make the incentives work required some adjustments. Heck, even some of the coordinators had to be retrained on how to use the reports that the others had been using for some time.

Soon, everyone was clamoring for those movie tickets and many were especially happy to have the ability to point with pride when they had a spectacular month.

Unfortunately, we forgot to bring Human Resources in on our plan, and about 18 months later they insisted we terminate the incentives since other departments had no such benefit. Never mind that the budget was quite modest (about $400 for each team for a year) and ours was the only department that had such easily measurable monthly goals. In all the excitement, we had simply forgotten the cardinal rule of coalition-building: keep your friends close, but your rivals and enemies closer.

We lost the incentives, but the metrics behind the incentives remained. This allowed managers to really understand what was being done in any given month and no longer had to rely on instinct or guess work as to whether a teleworking employee was goofing off.

The point of my story is simple: change is never easy, even when it is popular and grassroots-driven. Yet, the effort to bring about needed change is never without its benefits. After all, I can point quite directly to my role in that incentive program as the turning point in my career, as shortly thereafter I helped substitute for a manager during her medium-term hiatus, took on other projects, and eventually got promoted into a leadership role.

Don't be afraid of the work that bring about any sort of change may require. Change is never easy, but it can so easily be worth it.

Lesson 18: Question Your Ambitions

Take a moment and consider these two phenomena: highway hypnosis and the mid-life crisis.

Research has proven the existence of highway hypnosis. Imagine that you are riding home from work, at the same time of day as always, taking the same route, and listening to the same radio station. By the time you get home, you may not remember how you got there. Highway hypnosis is basically the result of short-term memory playing tricks on us. If it is not a significant new experience, our mind decides it is not worth investing in our long-term memory, so we end up forgetting it. We get a similar feeling when a significant anniversary in our work or persona lives comes up and we say, "Where did the years go?" as if we had been on autopilot the entire time.

As for the mid-life crisis, much has been made of this event in pop culture, particularly in how it could drive normally sane men to buy sports cars and get divorces. The idea there is much the same – at some point, you are given a chance to look back at all that you have done and you panic about the time you have lost.

I mention these two issues for a reason. They both represent the consequences of not paying attention to where your life is headed.

I learned the value of taking stock of your ambition and career path fairly early on.

As I mentioned earlier, I obtained my master's degree after two years on the job. Convinced that my real career was in politics, I did a major job search in the months after getting my degree. I even landed interviews on Capitol Hill. Yet, being a Democrat in 2004 was just bad timing.

After a year of trying, I realized I was getting close to the five-year mark that would entitle me to a lump sum pension check from the company. It no longer made sense for me to quit the current job. Shortly thereafter, I landed two different promotions and was making decent money, effectively pricing me out of a major career change.

After Obama's victory in 2008, I went through another bout of resume-printing, but was less energetic about making the effort. Around that same time, I took on new challenges and was being offered new opportunities for professional growth.

Soon enough, I was approaching 10 years at the company and I needed to either admit that my current day job was my accepted career, or I needed to make a change. Around that time, my employer created a position that amounted to my dream job, in that it combined subject matter expertise with training, management potential, and room to grow.

In effect, every few years I reexamined where I stood and I made a conscious decision about my ambitions. While I do sometimes lament that I am not a presidential speechwriter, like I had wanted, I am satisfied that I am in a job that I enjoy at a company I respect.

I think it is an extremely wise thing to question your ambitions from time to time. If you're off track, or find yourself craving different opportunities, it is better to fix matters as early as possible, so you do not end up in middle age cursing your lost youth and wondering where all the years have gone.

Lesson 19: Take Risks and Don't Give Up

Theodore Roosevelt once said, "It is impossible to win the great prizes of life without running risks."

At this fairly early point in your career, you've had a job for a while, perhaps received a promotion or two, and you've taken time to question your ambitions.

If your goals haven't changed by now, then it is certainly not the time to give up on them. Of course, to achieve them, you may have to do something uncomfortable, take an acceptable risk, or grab an opportunity a coworker had their eye on. It won't be easy. But then, if it were, it probably was not worth aiming for anyway.

By the time 2011 had arrived, I had blown past the 8-year mark at the company and the 5-year mark in the role of a coordinator. Despite some interesting challenges over the years, I was beginning to feel like I was no longer getting much out of working except a pay check. I also had not yet fully convinced myself that my prior political ambitions were not to be, so I was getting restless.

I think my coworkers may have noticed my frustrations. When it came time to re-elect me as grievance chair, I lost. Usually I'm disappointed by such an outcome, but I was thoroughly relieved. I was able to duck some work-related stress and perhaps move on to something better.

I had no idea how right that timing would be.

Not even two months later, a manager told me that the department was planning to create a new program manager role in quality assurance. The role would double-check the work of the coordinators, among other things. She told me to keep the news quiet, since nothing was final or official yet, but she also told me she thought I would be an ideal candidate for it. Sure enough, during that summer, such a position was announced.

I was ecstatic. That is, until I learned that my best friend, a fellow coordinator, was also interested. She had loads of experience, and filled a functionally similar role before.

I knew she really wanted it, and I did not want to stand in her way. A supervisory position was also opening up, and I would have preferred that to the quality role, since by then I was convinced that managing people is where my career was headed.

I took the risk of losing her friendship and applied anyway. It turns out that the department's leaders were looking for more technical work from the position and were hoping for someone who could make the job into something beyond the post-payment reviews my friend loved doing. So not only did my friend decide she did not want the job, but it turned out that I was a perfect fit and was offered it.

Somehow during that year, my ambitions had changed, just in time to take a risk and possibly land my dream job. How that happened is a journey I will not soon forget.

PART FOUR: GETTING YOUR DREAM JOB

"Everyone shines, given the right lighting. For some, it's a Broadway spotlight, for others, a lamplit desk." – Susan Cain

Lesson 20: What Is Your Dream Job?

Such a simple question, isn't it? Even when we are little, we think we know our answer: Astronaut. Sheriff. Doctor. Cowboy.

Yet, it can be a very difficult question to answer. Do you really know what you would like to do every day, day in and day out for the next 40 years? Have you considered everything that you have even some talent for? Are you prone to getting bored after a while?

Even if you could answer the question, and you could land that dream job, you might find out that you are actually wrong. Maybe the reality of being a photographer is too cash-poor for your taste. Maybe the life of a writer is too secluded. Maybe being a movie star sounds great, but the daily grind of auditions and rejections is too much to take.

Still, half the battle of getting your true dream job is to simply know what it is. After all, until you are honest with yourself about what you want, you will never find your dream job.

Rest assured, though, everyone has a dream job that can be found and obtained. As author Susan Cain said in the quote I opened this part of the book with, everyone shines; it is just a matter of finding the lighting that works for you.

I made the rash decision to move to D.C. because I thought I wanted to be involved in politics. I wasted several months looking for a job in part because I was not certain what exactly I was looking for, aside from something to pay the bills. Did I want to work on Capitol Hill? Did I want to work for lobbyists? Did I want to work in policy, or campaigns, or in speechwriting? I had no idea.

Not having a clear dream job made it easier for me to accept my day job as "good enough" for the next few years. While I still would not mind working for a Senator or for a President as their speechwriter, I know too many people now who worked on the Hill for low pay, long hours, and incredible stress, in attire that I despise. I know now that it is not likely to ever be something I do. That is actually okay, because I have a better sense of the kind of work I like doing, and it does not require having a politician for a boss.

Do you know what you want to do with your life? Do you know what it will take to get there?

Well, let's assume you have a sense of what you want, but are not entirely sure. There are some steps you should take to become better acquainted with yourself and your strengths, so you can be sure that what you perceive to be your dream job is actually a good fit.

These steps include increasing self-awareness, developing and refining a distinctive skill set, seizing opportunities as they arise, and not being afraid to gain and use knowledge for professional gain.

Lesson 21: Know Your Self

More often than not, conflicts in the workplace are driven by personality, not some parlor game of office politics. That is not to say that politics does not exist, and the higher up the ladder you get, the more you have to be mindful of it. But for most of us, we cannot dwell on things that cannot controlled, so we will set aside office politics for now.

At this point, you have chosen your adventure, found a job, and perhaps switched jobs or got promoted once or twice. You are still searching for that perfect opportunity to use your skills in pursuit of your passion: in other words, the dream job.

Some of you may never find it.

But I am here to help.

The first thing we need to do is get back to basics.

Are you an introvert?

That is pretty fundamental question. I could have lead off the book with this topic, but held off for a very simple reason – not all of us know for sure, and plenty of us have horrible memories of high school cliques and being type-cast based on our flaws. Truthfully, your search for the dream job may be most successful only after you have given yourself a chance to figure a few things out while working in a less than ideal job.

One of the first things worth figuring out are your dominant personality traits, as they can be helpful guides into what kind of activities you like and what kind of work settings are stimulating to you.

Myers-Briggs is a popular and influential personality assessment that categorizes people based on 4 binary axes, creating 16 different personality types. This level of detail and differentiation is why Myers-Briggs is my preferred measure of personality.

Of the 4 binary axes, the extrovert/introvert (E/I) dichotomy is perhaps the best-known and most consequential. Most of our personality at work is shown through our social interactions, leaving this dichotomy as the most obvious to people whom we are not particular close.

The extrovert draws his or her energy from people, from crowds, from social settings. Not all extroverts are the "life of the party" type, but all of them would rather spend their Friday nights at nightclubs with their friends than watching television alone. In work matters, the extrovert would prefer to be on project teams, perhaps cross-departmentally where they can network with strangers.

The introvert's energy is drained by such activities. They would rather spend their weekend reading a good book alone in the park than watching a football game from the 50-yard line. At work, they are lone wolfs and are likely champions of any move toward teleworking that keeps them safe at home.

Of course, those are broad outlines. There are exceptions. Some extroverts might prefer being at parties but not actually interact with anyone. Some introverts are the life of the party, but only for a small handful of close friends. Also, you might find yourself acting more like an extrovert in a smaller group and more like an introvert in a larger one.

In fact, most iterations of the Myers-Briggs test show results on a continuum from extrovert to introvert. It is not unheard of for your own results to vary from test to test, or to end up near the middle. I am very much in that camp – I have grown more extroverted as I've gotten older, yet I've also noticed that I retreat to more introverted behavior in large crowds of strangers. I also love public speaking, but get very nervous when I am not prepared. We will talk about situational behavior like this in a later lesson I learned.

What about the other behavior axes? The other three dichotomies are important dimensions in our personality, but their effects on the workplace are a bit more subtle.

There is the judgmental/perceptive (J/P) axis. This is the Odd Couple continuum, between neat freaks and slobs, between the list-checking obsessed and the live-and-let-live free spirits. Judgmental types are more organized, task-oriented, and tend to see the world in black and white. Perceptive types enjoy multi-tasking and love seeing the possibilities of any new project.

The sensing/intuitive (S/N) divide is better expressed by the Spock/Kirk partnership from Star Trek. Sensing types prefer reality, facts, specific information. Intuitive types prefer working with ideas, concepts, and "big picture" perspectives. This can sometimes be expressed as a divide between realist/pragmatic types and the idealist/creative types, but that might not be a perfect comparison.

The thinking/feeling (T/F) divide is also shown in Star Trek through the Spock/McCoy divide, and is a fairly straightforward expression of the role emotions play in one's behavior. A thinker might appear cold and logical and matter-of-fact, while a feeler is going to be very much concerned about morale.

As with the E/I axis, any of these divisions can get blurred over time, in specific situations, or simply because you are more complicated than can be expressed in these fashions.

For the record, my scores for the longest time end up in the INTJ category. This means I am a bit of an organized lone wolf who likes seeing the big picture and doesn't care to get too entangled in his own emotions. This rare personality combination is basically a self-confident bookworm. It was the results from these scores that lead me to assume and self-identify as an introvert.

Yet, in recent testing, I have also scored as an ENTJ, with a slight extroverted tendency and a J trait that has become a lot less pronounced. This makes sense, as my work requires more interaction with people and requires more juggling of multiple priorities (tasks better suited for the E's and P's of the world). Also, in my day job, I have to spend a lot of time digging around for the details I need (a task that an S would love) in order to support my N tendencies for wanting to see the longer-term trends. So, you might say that my personality has been drifting a bit as I get older.

Another thing to consider is that you may display different personality traits in different settings, or be judged as having a different trait than the test says. As I mentioned, I have found myself picking up more extroverted traits as I rise in the ranks, particularly in small groups or when I am familiar with the people or topic being discussed. Moreover, my coworkers have begun insisting that I am not an introvert at all, which might be a reflection of just how introverted my coworkers are.

Newer research has cast doubt on the dichotomy of the extrovert-introvert axis, by describing a class of "ambiverts" that consist of what I describe as "shy extroverts" and "outgoing introverts." After all, just because an extrovert likes being around people doesn't mean they aren't awkward with strangers or shy about their own vulnerabilities. Likewise, introverts may prefer to be alone, but that doesn't mean they are not welcome, lively additions at social gatherings. I know these blended traits exist, as my workplace has them in spades.

That is all just a way of saying that my personality, like yours, is fluid. Do not assume you are limited or bound by the results of these tests to be in jobs tailored to your dominant personality type. Instead, see taking a test like Myers-Briggs as a tool for building self-awareness of your own tendencies and reminding you of some of your workplace strengths.

These 4 categories yield 16 personality types, ranging from the INTJ result (which is often described as a strategist personality) to an ESFP (which is ideal for a life as a performer). There are a great number of books on how to handle these personalities or to find careers that match these personalities. You can Google them or do a search on Amazon.

So, whatever your personality type is, a good first step toward landing your dream job is for you to find out more about your personality, learn about what kind of successful jobs people with your personality have had, and find out in a general sense the types of personalities you will encounter from the people that can help you get your dream job.

This is especially important for introverts, who have a harder time dealing with people we do not know. Susan Cain advises in her manifesto for introverts that "in the long run, staying true to your temperament is key to finding work you love and work that matters" and I could not agree with her more.

Lesson 22: Know Your Niche

I hate sales, especially sales jobs that pay on commission. Fortunately, there are plenty of energetic, out-going people who can handle the grunt work of cold-calling strangers and networking the bejesus out of their Rolodex in order to make a sale. I hope I never have to relive those weekends I spent in high school trying to sell ads in our yearbook.

The reality of work today is not that simple. Even if we are not in sales, we are all selling something, all the time. We are selling ourselves, our talents, and our expertise.

The idealist in me hates the idea that we are increasingly living in a world dominated by networking, where "who you know" matters at least as much, if not more, than "what you know."

One way to combat this trend is to sell your "niche."

Niche is a term most often found in marketing, to describe a small, well-defined share of the marketplace.

To give you an example, let us consider Apple. Before the iPod, the company was a niche player in the computer business. Apple was best known for making high-end computers that artists would use because its interface was easier to navigate than DOS or early Windows, and had a more elegant design (both in its hardware and its software). This meant its computers were seen as an artist's device, a hipster's choice, and thus not something mainstream workers would want.

There are over 100 million working Americans. Even within our chosen fields, each individual's market share is tiny. To make matters worse, the competition is fierce. For any opportunity, you might be up against a dozen of your own clones – a dozen different people with very similar resumes.

How would you stand out?

How about by developing your own niche in the workplace marketplace?

It is not enough to be self-aware of your own personality type. No one ever puts their Myers-Brigg results on their resume or cover letter.

Instead, you have to reach beyond those personality quirks of yours to define and refine the elements that truly set you apart from everyone else.

For example, perhaps you are a registered nurse. There are plenty of nurses out there seeking new opportunities to use their skills. Now, maybe one of your quirks is that you are a bit of a tech nerd and are fascinated by recent advancements. You could recognize that as a niche and build your career around medical technology. That way, the next time a nursing position comes up and you are competing with a dozen other people with similar years of experience, your background in med tech will stand out.

Once you know your niche, you have to make sure other people know it, too. In other words, you have to use it to build a brand.

Lesson 23: Build Your "Brand"

Branding is one of those cutesy marketing words that somehow made it mainstream. This happened much to my chagrin, not because I disapprove of the concept, but because a lot of douche bags and hipsters have helped to create a bit of social stigma around the term's use. Yet, that happens quite a lot in today's society – every good suggestion taken to an extreme either becomes a rule for a lifestyle (a healthy skepticism became a dry sense of irony among hipsters) or gets attached to something to such a degree that the rest of us want to puke (a frat boy trying to act cultured for his smart dates created the very first "douche bag" that is now epitomized by the character of Schmidt on television's New Girl).

Yet, personal branding exists whether we are conscious of it or not. Other people have pre-conceived notions of who you are and what you are about it. This is why the cliché phrase that "politics is perception" exists, because how you are perceived matters. So why not become more conscious of that and try to take control of those perceptions? That is what I think of when I think of branding.

It is not enough to know who you are and what niche you might be able to fill at your company or in society generally. You also have to bend your reputation so that it matches your intended niche.

For example, if you want to be known as the nicer, more outgoing employee among a set of other similarly skilled, hard-working colleagues, you run the risk of also being seen as a social butterfly if you are never at your own desk getting work done. You have to find a way to enhance your perceived strengths without creating more baggage.

For example, the registered nurse who built a niche as an expert in medical devices has such a narrow niche that it practically brands itself. She would just need to be careful that she not be seen as lacking in clinical knowledge if she ever wanted to get back into traditional nursing.

In my own experience, I had a colleague that had a similar interest in program development who worked very diligently in testing computer systems and often had a hard time coaxing user requirements out of us to give to the programmers. He also had a hard time following up on small issues, and found it difficult to explain certain changes to our computer systems. That left him respected, but not exactly someone people went to with their problems.

I tried to avoid those issues by showing our coworkers that I could make changes to our reports in a way that made their lives easier, and if I could add a pop of color, graphics, or fun to our proceedings, I would.

After all, I intended my workplace niche to be that of a creative nerd. I built a brand to match through my hobbies, my personal website and Twitter account, and the projects I took on. Once I had an office and people started coming to me with questions, I began offering them sweets like jellybeans to make them more comfortable. If I couldn't be a popular or fun person by personality or career choice, I'd at least try to be more approachable than the average manager.

When further changes took place and I was set to take on supervising a team for the first time, the staff that came to me with their questions had concerns that I might not be able to help them as much as before. Seems like my branding worked, didn't it?

Lesson 24: Be Creative

In many ways, the 21st century is an iPad world of Apple's creation; we are only living in it. In this high-tech age of global capitalism, the future belongs to the most nimble-minded of companies, the ones that foster innovation from within and are not afraid to think "outside the box" in finding new ways to generate value.

That macro view of modern economics is largely true on the micro, individual level as well. Even in the most risk-averse, tradition-bound of corporate cultures, there is an increasing acceptance of trying new things.

Whether your dream job involves a promotion to the big corner office or making it big in Hollywood, being creative in some form or another is going to be a career accelerator.

The best part is that creativity is not limited to the artsy things we learned in school. Creative thinking is now linked to a wide variety of fields, from scientific research to marketing to statistics to data analysis to information security.

Creativity can be as simple as finding a simpler way to run a report, or improving a work process. Or, in my case, creativity was using our existing queries to build new ones that looked at the data in new ways.

For example, we have a "pending code" system of setting reminder flags on a beneficiary's record so that any user can look up the beneficiary and know what documentation was needed by the processing staff. We also set goals of following up on any pending code that was set more than 30 days earlier. At the same time, we knew from anecdotal evidence (complaints coming in to our Call Center) that some employees were not as attentive to their cases as they should be.

Me being me, I wanted to know if there was a correlation between the two. I created a new performance measure that we call "cases needing action." It is a simple percentage of cases with pending codes past due for at least 30 days over total number of cases assigned to each processor. If John Doe has 3 past-due pend codes and 100 total cases, he has a "cases needing action" rate of 3%.

Sure enough, when we first ran this report, many of the processors receiving complaints had high rates of pending codes that were past due.

We now use that measurement in our routine reporting of performance, and have set a goal of keeping a lid on it of no more than 10% each month. Personally, I think that is being generous; after all, what we are talking about are cases that are already past-due by an entire month, and in an era of shrinking work volume, there shouldn't be any excuse for someone to be behind by that much in their work. Fortunately for the staff, I do not get the final word on that kind of decision.

Being creative is quite useful, even in small and banal ways. It is a great skill to have in solving problems, and solving problems is a key part of any job, especially the higher you move up in the career ladder.

Lesson 25: Seize Opportunities

For most us, landing our dream job will not come easy. We will not be handed it on day one. We will need to work for it. This is doubly true if your dream job involves a promotion at your current organization.

So how do you convince your boss and other superiors that you deserve the job you covet? The easiest thing you can do is to seize any opportunity that you can, by either taking advantage of the opportunities you are given, or by creating your own.

Let me tell you about a failure to take advantage of an opportunity given to you on a silver platter. A coworker of mine had ambitions to move up to Assistant Director, but he lacked supervisory experience because his current role involved tackling projects of a particularly technical nature. When his colleague went on maternity leave, he was asked to substitute for her as the supervisor of an employee. This was his chance to prove that he had the skills needed in an AD despite not having much experience overall. After several months, the colleague returned and he resumed his regular work. I did not even realize he was supervising the employee until after the colleague returned, and I was not the only one. In a way, this was a missed opportunity, particularly if he had done more than complete timesheets. If he had taken a chance to get more involved in the employee's work and resolve any issues the employee may have had under the other supervisor, then he would have shown himself quite adept at handling people and would have relieved the department of a long-festering issue.

An example of successfully seizing an opportunity that you yourself created can be found in my involvement in the incentive rewards. I already discussed this project in Lesson 17, so I will not repeat myself.

Let me give you another example, one whose outcome is not yet determined. A coworker who is well-liked among the staff was given the opportunity to be a coordinator for a team with whom he was already familiar. He was thought to be a good complement to the new manager for that team, since he had people skills the manager lacked. If he could successfully partner with that manager to develop the team into a high-functioning success story, then his presumed skills would be validated and it would be a feather in his cap if he ever wanted to be a future manager. He did not take full advantage of that opportunity, in part because the Union saw his potential and tried filling his free time with other work for their own benefit. Now, as promotional opportunities are opening up, he has a track record he can trumpet, but is it as strong as it could have been?

If you really do want your career to move higher, do not let an opportunity pass you by without at least recognizing the potential loss. You do not want to be seen a hungry for a promotion, but you also do not want to be left with an empty resume when it comes time for that big interview.

Lesson 26: Expand Your Scope of Responsibilities

Whether you wanted to be a manager, or a well-respected expert in your field, or are still stuck trying to figure everything out, you will always find colleagues who are quite content with doing the minimum. You may also find superiors who are too busy to finish everything on their agenda, and may trust you enough to delegate work. If you learned the previous lesson, you seized those opportunities and may even be revisiting lesson #15 (that being the best at your job is okay).

There is something related to all of this, a lesson that I learned after my promotion to management: if you expand the scope of your responsibilities, you could become indispensable to the higher-ups, and can even find yourself enjoying your job even more.

When I first took on the job of quality manager, the job was envisioned as primarily an in-house auditor that looked at cases already paid to ensure we were doing things correctly. It was a worthwhile role, especially when you add to it the ability to look at the big picture and see if the errors are clustered around one topic or one individual.

A couple months in, a suggestion was made that instantly transformed what I did. The department director thought it would be a good idea if the training manager and I collaborated on a question-and-answer session where staff could come to us with their difficult cases and we would solve it together as a group.

The sessions fairly quickly morphed into monthly technical training, often on topics not covered in the regular training staff received when they become processors.

Now, two years later, I have a training certificate from the American Society of Training & Development and will take over the training function for our department when our training manager leaves the company in the summer.

I could not be happier. I'll get into the benefits of training in the next three lessons, but for now just let me say that if I had not agreed to the expanded responsibility, I might not have found an element of the job that I so thoroughly enjoy, and which has given me a skill-set that the department needed and that would help me wherever my career takes me later.

Of course, the risk you take in expanding your responsibility is that you may become over-extended. Work-related stress could set in, and your performance could suffer. If you can strike that balance, though, there is no telling what can happen.

Lesson 27: Knowledge is Power

This is a lesson that reverberates throughout this book, but this simple phrase is so simple that it can be easily overlooked. So let me say that again:

Knowledge is power.

You cannot hope to obtain your dream job – whether it is a concert pianist, a presidential speechwriter, or a veterinarian for homeless kittens – without knowledge. It's that powerful.

In one sense, this lesson could be found in Machiavelli's *The Prince* or Robert Greene's *The 48 Laws of Power*. Hopefully, my choice in references gave you a sense of the connotation I am going for.

As powerful as knowledge can be in enabling your talents and skills, it can also have a significant effect on your influence in the workplace, for good and for bad.

For example, what if you have knowledge that two employees are competing for a position that is not even open yet? While you may not be in a position to directly influence the outcome of that competition, just knowing that the jockeying is occurring will better inform you of the subtext of any dysfunction occurring in the project on which the three of you are working. Knowing that subtext will allow you to better consider how you respond to the dysfunction: will you let it continue? Will you take sides, knowing you might be drawn into the fight? Will you inform a superior?

I learned this lesson along the way toward my dream job, without fully realizing it until the interview.

The job, which I mentioned earlier, was a new position at the organization that would manage quality. It would require expertise in the Plan rules, the ability to use a specific program for running lists and reports, some knowledge of statistics, and the ability to make presentations to a varied audience.

We, the applicants, understood the job to be primarily a kind of in-house auditor for our department, checking up on quality to preemptively fix mistakes that the real auditors might have found. In that respect, any number of people with experience at the company could probably do just fine. However, as we all interviewed, at least one applicant realized the job would not be a good fit for her, as she was not as strong in creating and running reports.

Who was strong in that? Me. Over the years, I developed an interest in that program and in using it to find the answers to certain questions we had about our caseload. Over time, I ended up writing most of the reports that the staff use regularly. And now, if I won the promotion, I would have the chance to write additional reports for my own needs and interests.

There were other areas when my knowledge won out. I lead a pilot program to build incentives around our performance metrics. I was given a chance to supervise a team while their manager was out. I even had coursework in college on statistics and research methods.

I cannot say whether any of those were decisive factors in my winning the position, but they certainly put me in a better position to win that I would have otherwise, since I had less experience with the organization than most of my competition.

In a meritocracy, mere breadth of experience is not enough. Success based on merit requires something more, some proof that you alone bring something to the table that others cannot. Here, knowledge is power. Anyone aspiring to rise above needs to either eliminate the skills gap between them and their competition, or find that extra something they can learn that will simply blow everyone else away.

You will never lose by learning something new.

Lesson 28: Share Your Knowledge

In learning the previous lesson, I learned this one. Yes, knowledge is power. Yet, the temptation we all run into when believing knowledge is power is seeing knowledge as something to hoard, as if it were a precious gold ring stolen by Hobbits. Yet, its truest power comes from being able to transfer that knowledge to someone else.

The lesson I had to learn when developing my own knowledge-based power was that anyone can be a trainer, regardless of what the org chart says, and that sharing your knowledge is as important as having it to begin with.

If you know something unique, you can share that knowledge with someone else. In the act of sharing it, you have become a trainer, regardless of your title or pay.

Do not shy away from that opportunity.

If your aspiration is to become a manager, for example, much of your time may be spent on coaching low-performing employees. There is a fine line between coaching and training, and we'll get into that a little bit more in Part Five of the book.

Alternatively, you may discover you love training and want that to be your profession. It can happen to anyone, even if we were not all education majors in college.

Sadly, as a profession, trainers suffer the most from budget cuts, disrespect, and frustratingly vague expectations. It is not an easy career path unless you are fully committed to the role and are prepared to readily switch employers at the first sign of a layoff.

That said, there is a lot to be gained by having experience as a trainer. You interact with your coworkers on a different level than the org chart might require. You gain respect through sharing your expertise. If you do the job well, you might even be seen as a potential leader by your superiors, who are always on the lookout for new talent within the organization.

Whether or not you want the title, there is a lot to be gained by learning how to train other people. Transferring your knowledge is just another way to make you valuable.

Lesson 29: Learn Something New Every Day

In the previous lessons, I talked about how knowledge is power. It is only logical that another lesson learned is an extension of that lesson: that one should be learning something new every day.

This does not have to be a something big, like learning a foreign language or working toward an advanced degree. It can be as simple as learning more about your coworkers so that you can be a better colleague. If you are not learning something new every day, you're doing it wrong.

That, to me, is what lifelong learning is really all about – the commitment to building your knowledge and your skills, no matter how small the achievement or how big the audacious goal. If you can learn something new every day, you will take that next step toward discovering yourself and picking up the tools you need in order to realize your goal of obtaining that elusive "dream job."

When I was a teenager, I had a pretty linear mindset about learning: I would suffer through my high school's International Baccalaureate program; finish college as quickly as possible; get a master's degree, if not a PhD; declare victory, and start a career.

At the time I got to graduate school, my views on this still had not changed much. I had moved to D.C. just after turning 21, so you might want to excuse my naïveté on my youth and inexperience.

Two years into working at my day job, I was frustrated in my search for my dream job – at that point, it was to work on Capitol Hill for a Democrat that I liked. An opportunity came up to get promoted, and I finally realized a lesson I would repeatedly learn or remind myself of over the years: you have to learn something new every day.

In this particular case, I could use the new position to learn more about ERISA, the package of federal laws governing pensions. Surely, I figured, knowledge of a particular law could be a boost to my non-lawyer resume in landing that dream job. It would also prove to be a challenging role, which helped keep the job-search frustrations at bay by giving me something else on which to focus my energies.

Later, having discovered that my career goals had changed, I decided I needed to strengthen my value to the company if I were ever to get promoted to manager. After years of maximizing my value by challenging myself to do better in my current job, I decided the easiest way to go further was to make a splash in adding to my professional and educational credentials.

So I took the lifelong learning concept and made it a little more literal, by signing up for the first in a series of self-study exams leading to a designation as a retirement plans associate, which is part of a broader professional certification sponsored by the Wharton School of Business at the University of Pennsylvania.

Not only would I be providing more value to the company by expanding my knowledge of federal rules that govern our retiree benefit plans, but I would also be adding to the list of skills I could transfer to another company should I ever leave the organization in pursuit of my career.

This was a classic win-win scenario.

Sure, a degree program or a professional certification requires a lot more work than learning about your coworkers, but it also has greater rewards.

That does not mean you should only focus on the big-ticket items here. There is nothing wrong with thinking small when it comes to lifelong learning. Just like dieting, often the commitment is easier if the commitment is more manageable. The point is to recognize the value of knowledge and the value of never giving up on obtaining as much knowledge as you can. It will help you in your career, and may very well help launch you into your dream job.

PART FIVE: MANAGING A TEAM

"The conventional definition of management is getting work done through people, but real management is developing people through work." ~ Agha Hasan Abedi

Lesson 30: Managing Is A Learned Skill

A lot of people scheme and conspire to move up the ranks at their day jobs, hoping to become a manager. For some, the motivation behind the ambition is pay and other perks. For others, it's the perceived prestige.

In fact, many people perceive the role of a manager as being their "dream job" for all of the perceived rewards, without thinking much of how to get there or the costs that might be involved in attaining or keeping the job.

Along the way, I decided that I really did want to become a manager. Sure, I still wanted to be creative, either through my writing or as a trainer, but I knew my career endgame at my day job was to be a manager. And just as I was turning 30, I was given the opportunity to be manager of a program, as a clear stepping stone toward becoming a manager of people.

You might be surprised to discover that there is no "on" switch for becoming a good manager. You do not unlock hidden powers, discover hidden talents, or win instant respect. Yes, you might move from a cubicle into an office, get business cards, and have a team reporting their timesheets to you, but there is real work ahead to earn the title you have already been given.

Sure, your bosses may think highly of you. After all, they promoted you. However, now you have to prove that they were right to give you a chance. Now you needed to earn their respect by throwing yourself into the work. My best advice on this front is to try to avoid causing too much drama. You can and should keep your own boss informed of issues on the team, but you should also be mindful of his or her own busy schedule and limit your reliance on them for only the things that truly matter, even if it means learning to not sweat the small things yourself.

As a new manager, you also have to earn the respect of your new peers, many of whom may feel threatened by your rise or didn't see you as deserving. Here, again, the best advice is to minimize drama. However, in this case, you could lean on your colleagues for advice; it will respect their experience and show them that you value their judgment, even if you do not always follow it.

The hardest task of a new manager, and one that I am still struggling with, is the slow realization that you are no longer responsible for the execution of the day-to-day details of the work. Instead, you are responsible for the people who execute that work. Letting go of that direct connection to the work we do will be especially difficult if you were promoted partly on your strength in doing that work.

If you are not careful, the manager who cannot let go of the details of the work will find themselves micro-managing their team to the point of needless stress and drama. Yet, you also cannot be so oblivious of that work that you have no control of your team. That is a delicate balance you must strike, one that even the best of managers will have a hard time maintaining.

If you are successful, however, you could find yourself helping out the department or the company in a more strategic capacity, as you begin to see how to make changes at a higher level. That is where some of the benefits of being a manager really lie.

Lesson 31: Emotional Intelligence

I am not a fan of corporate training. I am used to education being either knowledge-based or very specific and practical. Spending a couple hours or a couple days away from my office to talk with strangers in vague general terms about struggles with a skill or a problem back at work can feel like a waste of time. That is especially the case when the trainer does a lot of silly games and embarrassing icebreakers.

Even so, ice breakers and strangers come with the territory for off-site classes, and I accept that. My real beef with these training courses is the repetition in so many of them around the same handful of ideas, often tweaked and repackaged slightly differently.

One of the new trends in management training that I do like is this notion of an "emotional" form of intelligence on par with the nominal, more academic form of intelligence. You could also describe this as the "street smarts vs. book smarts" debate you may have seen played out in high school. Despite that analogy, I see validity in this latest training fad, especially in the context of leading a team.

David Rybak wrote in *Putting Emotional Intelligence to Work*, that "emotional intelligence is best defined as the ability to use your awareness and sensitivity to discern the feelings underlying interpersonal communications, and to resist the temptation to respond impulsively and thoughtlessly, but instead to act from receptivity, authenticity, and candor."

Just as with other trends or fads in management training, emotional intelligence can be broken down into four parts or key attributes: self-awareness leading to self-management, social-awareness, and relationship management.

We have covered several different elements of self-awareness in this book already, and will cover several more shortly. The better you know your own self, the more skilled you will get in controlling your worst impulses and in understanding others. With self-control and being empathetic, you will find more effective relationships and a greater degree of influence.

Other elements usually covered in emotional intelligence training programs include active listening and SMART goals, which are not unique to EI but are useful for managers to keep in mind.

Active listening requires the listener to absorb what is said, ask questions, paraphrase what has been said, agree on something, and indicate appreciation for the speaker taking the time to raise the issue being discussed. Active listening gives at least the appearance of empathy. This is especially helpful in difficult conversations, but could turn quite clunky in more every-day situations.

Unlike active listening, which at least has an application in emotional intelligence, the training that tries to package SMART goals into the same session is probably doing you a disservice. SMART goals (specific, measurable, ambitious, realistic, timely) are important in performance management, and can be used if you are trying to train yourself to use EI more, but its inclusion is indirect at best.

One thing that does not get addressed enough, though, is trust. Trust is a key emotion at work, and any breach of trust hurts employee morale which hurts productivity which in turn hurts the company.

For fans of alliteration, the folks at the American Management Association defined the elements of trust as including continuity, commonality, caring, communication, and competence. Trust has to be ongoing, based on some shared interest, with a real sense of sympathy, where either side can speak their mind freely without fear of the other screwing things up.

As far as that final element of trust – competence – goes, there are four types, in ascending order or value: unconscious incompetence, conscious incompetence, conscious competence, and unconscious competence. That is, if you are incompetent and you don't even know it, you may not be able to change and that is bad. On the other hand, being competent without being conscious of it means you are spending less time and energy on it and can do other things.

That is why some of our most successful counselors and managers have a hard time passing on tips for success, because they may not know what they are doing right – yet the time they save allows them to be more productivity, which is not at all a bad thing.

A good manager has many of the same attributes as someone with strong emotional intelligence, but we often describe them differently: self-awareness, maintaining a list of personal goals, developing alliances with others in leadership roles, and aligning daily tasks and personal goals with the company's agenda. The similarity between the two is why EI is one of the hot new trends in management, even if EI has been overhyped for offices and situations where emotional awareness is an unnecessary distraction (think medical labs or a hub of computer programmers).

This is why I put emotional intelligence here in the management section. If you have no aspirations for leading a team, or your job has little social interaction with your coworkers, I can see why it is not worth studying. But for everyone else, it is an important lesson, especially as a lesson in the importance of self-awareness.

There are plenty of books out now about emotional intelligence, and I would recommend you pick up any of them if you are interested in learning more about this topic.

Lesson 32: Your Personality at Work

When I searched for my dream job, one of the lessons I learned was to define my personality and find the kind of jobs that align with that personality. A very similar lesson must be learned with respect to being in management: your leadership style.

I became cognizant of one's leadership style being important while attending corporate training. One of the most-repeated (and thus my least-favorite) topics was a sort of truncated pop-psychology in the form of reducing personalities into 4-quadrant groupings.

Business schools are so fond of the 4-quadrant system that they have a long list of available paradigms that all generally express the same idea: Birkman Personality Activity, your True Color, the Romans' Body Humors, the 4 Elements (fire/water/earth/air), the Whole Brain Model by Ned Hermann, the Human Nature Model by Paul Lawrence and Nitin Nohria, the model championed by Anthony Gregory in Adult's Guide to Style, the DISC formulation favored by the American Management Association, and an alternate favored by David Merrill and Roger Reid. Beyond these, there are alternate dressings of these same models based on the quirks of the presenter. I remember one class used DISC but grouped people by animals that suggested that personality trait.

Here is a summary of how each of these models condenses the 16 personality types of Myers-Briggs into 4 work-relevant personalities:

The Director. This individual is more interested in tasks than in people, and is more interested in getting it done quickly than necessarily getting it perfect. They are the bosses who bark orders but rarely stick around to see it through. If they are new to the company, they can be a bit like a bull in a china shop, wanting to put their own stamp on things. They are used to being in charge and/or getting their way. If they are not yet in charge, they at least do not want their time wasted on minutia – they prefer to get the gist of your message in a sound bite fashion and then get back to what they were doing. Naturally, most CEOs can be found here.

The Influencer. This person also wants to see things done quickly, but is also socially active in the workplace. They are great at persuasion; they will use their knowledge of their coworkers to get what they want. They are also the ones worried about morale, so throwing office parties and making work fun is high on their priority list. Naturally, a lot of trainers and the better-liked managers end up in this quadrant.

The Co-Worker. I name this group this way because most formulations of the four-quadrant zone show this to be where the bulk of American workers are. The Co-Worker is not worried about the task to be done nearly as much as they are worried about supporting one another. They will ask how your weekend went and how the kids are doing. They generally dislike change, especially if it threatens their jobs. They see themselves as part of one or more teams, even if the team is not formally organized by Management, and will help their teammates get the work done.

The Perfectionist. This person is focused on getting the task done well, often to the exclusion of everything else. They prefer working alone, and will often reject teamwork (or do the team's work all by themselves) and will skip the office parties. They will get the task done right the first time, even if it takes them a long time to finish.

Every office has these four types, if not to the extremes I described. I would avoid getting caught up too much in the terminology or trying to figure out what group you are in. Depending on the testing method used, you could end up in any or all of them. Indeed, I was once an owl (i.e., the perfectionist), but have also scored as the co-worker type, and yet my dream job involves the work of influencers.

Meanwhile, as I mentioned, most of the models that use the four types admit that a majority of employees are in the co-worker type. This gives you a sense that every office has a similar dynamic, but it does not do enough to adequately describe what you might face. An office of energetic, party-animal sales and marketing people is going to be a very different office than one full of accountants, even if both offices have a perfectionist or a pushy boss.

So why is it so important to understand these kinds of workplace personalities? Well, even if you are the boss, you may have to supervise someone with a Director kind of attitude. How do you handle that person? Perceiving them as a Director, you will know that this employee prefers that you be straight forward and give them the gist without all the background information. Yet, not every employee will have that attitude. You will have to learn to be flexible with your approach, and recognize that your style can and will have to change in order to be the best possible leader for your team.

Lesson 33: Leadership Styles Should Help the Employees

Just to warn you, even though I did say I was annoyed with corporate training's obsession with most four-quadrant models, there is one model that is useful for this lesson, and therefore is worth discussing.

A good leader, even the popular trainer or manager in the influencer quadrant, is aware of their leadership style. Everyone has a default setting, and the better leaders add an element of dynamism to it that is otherwise called situational leadership.

The four-quadrant model on situational leadership describes four essential styles of leadership as well as the kind of situations where each style is warranted. The model is based on two axes: directive vs. supportive behavior.

In stage one, a purely *directing* style shows high directive and low supportive behavior by the manager. This is the bossiest of bossy styles – telling someone exactly what to do, how to do it, and when it is needed by. This style is best used when the employee's skills are low, otherwise it could be interpreted as a bit smothering. (This is similar to the Director style of workplace personality, and predictably can be the least popular way of managing people, particularly those with experience.)

In stage two, *coaching*, you are still deciding what gets done, but you involve the employee in a discussion of the task and why it is needed. This style is best used when skills are low and commitment is shaky; but you should only use it after you have built some trust and a relationship with the employee and want to see them improve.

In stage three, as the employee's skills improve, you shift toward *supporting* behavior. There is a discussion of the task to do, but you let them decide how to get it done. This style is particularly good to use with employees who have potential, even if they do not see it yet.

Finally, by stage four, the employee's skill and commitment are reaching a peak. Your trust in their ability to get it done is now high enough that you can *delegate* the task entirely to them, perhaps only setting the deadline and letting them figure out the details. (This can be the hardest leadership style to develop, as many managers like to have at least some direct involvement in the work for which they are responsible.)

All of us have a default style. The Director types mentioned earlier run the risk of being stuck largely in stage one, setting the tone by being a bit too much of a micromanager. A trainer is a coach by default. A hands-on manager may spend most of their time supporting their employees. A manager with a lot on their agenda, or with a strong team of professionals, might default to delegating the work.

Some problems faced by managers could be solved by tweaking their style. For example, is an employee slacking off? Perhaps you delegated too much and need to support or coach the employee back to full performance rather than waiting to catch them in act that can land them in a meeting with HR.

When I became a manager of a team, I was juggling all the tasks I handled before as well as all the work of leading that team. Luckily for me, my team was professional and largely ran on auto-pilot. Early on, though, I did have a challenge: one employee was underperforming.

I was taught in these management trainings that there are essentially three types of employees – poor performers, star performers, and the middle. Poor performers typically, but erroneously, take up a disproportionate amount of a manager's time. The typical manager's default instinct is to manage each crisis as it arises, and so we tend to focus our energy on the poor performers. Star performers, on the other hand, need none of our help.

So how should I have handled a poor performer in light of the leadership styles I just mentioned? It was easy. Chances are that the star performer among your employees is also a Co-Worker or an Influencer type who wants the team to succeed. Delegate to the star performer the task of working with the poor performer. That way, you can shift your focus to being an Influencer, coaching or supporting the middle-ground employees who could, if prompted, become star performers.

The lesson here is one of self-awareness. Know the dynamics of your office, know your own default leadership style, and be mindful of the kinds of situations that require a shift in your default setting.

Lesson 34: Maintain Priorities and Avoid Crises

An earlier lesson I had learned as an employee was to pick my battles wisely, raising issues only when I thought they were truly important because the higher-ups simply did not have time for silliness.

Now, as a manager, I had to learn the flip-side of that lesson. That is, I needed to learn to better manage my time so I could achieve everything that was expected of me. One consequence was learning to not sweat the small stuff.

Consider the type of manager who monitors your check-in, lunch, and check-out times. Unless you are on an assembly line, in a call center, or have an attendance problem, this level of micromanagement is not effective. It is stressful for the employee. It also requires a lot of time and energy on the part of the manager, time that could be better spent on more important matters than docking you for being less than 5 minutes late coming back from lunch.

"Sweating the small stuff" is also a kind of leadership style that can cause more problems than it solves, depending on the kind of team you have.

When their supervisor left, a team was transferred to me as part of a minor reorganization. Suddenly I had to do my own work, as well as the work of the departing manager. I could have continued her past practices of closely monitoring inflows, production, and quality. She had a lot of success with that hands-on approach. However, I did not have the luxury of time that that approach would have required. I had to make a choice in how I would manage my own time. I decided I did not want to make any sudden changes in how the team functioned, and I decided I would let the high-functioning team basically run on its own until they needed my help.

My decision with that team was hardly perfect, as some issues persisted that a more direct approach might have avoided. That happens. The trade-off in letting small things go is that you give the team room to make mistakes. Sometimes, that is all you can do in order to keep you and your team as close to on track as you can.

Lesson 35: Performance Reviews Are Hard

Why are performance reviews so difficult? Dr. Chris Wright, CEO of Reliant, explained once that performance reviews are hard because even the fairest system is still going to be seen as unfair by at least some employees.

I can agree with that, and if I were writing this book from an employee's perspective, I could probably write a whole section on evaluations that were done poorly and weigh the various alternative systems.

However, for this lesson, I wanted to share my experience as a manager having to deliver performance reviews for the first time.

Every year, our company does performance evaluations for our staff. This ritual is not tied to pay raises and is separate from any ongoing disciplinary matters. In my department in particular, the ritual often comes after 12 consecutive monthly meetings with each person where the manager is supposed to discuss their most recent performance.

In theory, performance reviews should be quick and easy.

In reality, performance reviews are hard.

I learned this lesson in the summer after taking over one of our processing teams. Maybe it was because these were my first evaluations. Maybe it was because I was taking the evaluation forms so seriously. Maybe it was because they only allowed 3 rankings (exceeds expectations, meets expectations, and needs improvement). Maybe it was all of the above.

This was an unexpected lesson to learn. After all, our department has a lot of measurable, quantifiable performance measures that are recorded monthly. Surely I could just take the average of each and use that to inform my evaluation. Well, unfortunately, my team was the last to incorporate those measures. Also, the evaluation requires us to consider non-quantifiable measures, such as the employee's dependability and communication skills.

I was one of the first managers to finish, but I still took the better part of two solid weeks writing the six evaluations.

I wanted to be fair, accurate, and thorough, especially for those I was giving a less than stellar rating. Even on my star performers, I wanted to be frank with them on the small areas they had to work on.

Of course, not everything went smooth. One employee felt strongly that their one "meets expectations" (the rest were "exceeds") should have been rated higher, even after I explained that I took their interactions with team members into account and it was really their only area to work on.

No matter how hard you try, you may not please everyone, even when the evaluations are more of a formality than anything else. And if you try, you will find yourself spending whole days or weeks writing the perfect essays – only to have a difficult conversation about what you wrote.

That's why performance reviews are so hard.

Lesson 36: "Face Time" Has Value

The higher up you go in your career, the less it matters what your subject matter expertise has been. At a certain level, you are a manager of people, regardless of who the people are or what it is they do. Of course, in many fields, such as accounting or legal, it helps if the top guy in charge is also highly qualified. What I mean, though, is that your next promotion may have more to do with office politics than with qualifications.

"Face time" was lampooned in Dilbert, but in many ways it is a very real thing. You have to get noticed to get ahead, and if the decision-makers don't recognize you, it can be a very bad thing.

I recently heard from a fellow manager that some manager in another department "had no idea" who I was or what I did, and he acted like I should be concerned that my achievements were not better known throughout the company. Yet, I shrugged off the worry. This third person was in a department I had no interest in joining and frankly I did not see how his knowledge of our department would or should matter to me.

What mattered to me was that my boss appreciated my work, that the department director knew my value, and that I continued to do all the things that had served me well and could position me for the future. I had just been promoted and had time to consider my next move.

Later, I was asked to attend a meeting with our Executive Director, the department director, and my boss. The meeting was about a vacant position on my team. Due to predictions of inclement weather, I was the only one from our department who could attend in person; the others were called into a conference line. I felt fairly strongly that I had to attend in person; not only is a meeting with the Executive Director a rare occasion, but I thought it would just look bad if she could attend in person but no one else did, especially when the meeting was to discuss an important issue for our department. We came to a consensus on how to handle the vacancy, so I left the meeting satisfied. One of the lawyers that attended told me afterwards that she thought I represented the Department well, which was just icing on the cake for me.

When you have "face time" like that, you have to make good use of the opportunity; it would be silly to waste such a rarity. You should avoid, however, being the kind of person who obsesses about their reputation to the exclusion of doing anything to merit that reputation. Instead, you should do your job and do it well, and let the work speak for itself. Office politics is a game rife with danger that is often just not worth the trouble.

While I am on the subject of face time, the flip side of this issue is the idea of "living for the weekend" or, as many people see it, "living for the personal day."

I mentioned once to a co-worker how many vacation hours I have saved up (nearly 3 months' worth), and was met with a gasp, and then a mix of disappointment and amazement. It seems that most of the people she knew were always running out of vacation and sick leave, some even resorting to asking for "leave without pay" when they needed it.

Now, for some people, I can totally understand that. Young children, sick relatives and other health problems are all valid reasons for having to miss work, and if you are unlucky, you could end up using up a meager allotment of vacation very quickly for non-vacation reasons. Likewise, if you earn enough and have the itch to travel, I can easily see you taking advantage of your leave as much as possible to go on exotic vacations. However, as a young, single guy who rarely gets sick and has no enthusiasm for air travel, I've just not had much of reason to use leave for any reason. So I have just let the leave accumulate even as my colleagues struggle to save up any at all.

Flexible scheduling and tele-working also play a role in my lack of vacations. I work in the office 8 calendar days per pay period; I work at home 1 day; and have the other 5 days off. This does not count holidays, office closures, or any minor use of leave. If I had to come into the office 10 days per pay period, I might be more prone to taking days off because I might get sick more often or just have too much stress.

All the same, I make use of my time in the office. I've minimized my teleworking, and I track all my projects so I can cross them off my list as they are finished. This helps ensure that I follow-through on projects as well as giving me a sense of achievement when the project is over. A lot of my work requires interaction with staff, including training sessions, so the staff knows what I do.

If I were doing projects by myself and telecommuted a lot, I would not blame anyone for not thinking much of what I did, because they just wouldn't have any way of knowing. In fact, when I became a manager, I told the department director that I could not handle the work in such a fashion – even if most of my days are spent alone in my office, I wanted staff members to be able to come to me when they had questions, and they could only do that if I were visibly available.

Just because one manager in a different department on a different floor has no idea who I am doesn't mean I haven't made use of face time in a way that makes sense for me. Yes, it has perhaps enabled me to be a bit of a workaholic at the cost of never taking a vacation even though I have the time, but I'd like to think that, to the people that matter most in my own department, I am valuable, if not indispensable. And that is all that matters.

PART SIX: GOING FORWARD

"The best thing about the future is that it comes only one day at a time." ~ Abraham Lincoln

Lesson 37: Skills – Practice Them Or Lose Them

In college, I learned the importance of clubs and hobbies for networking and refining my skills. In my day job, I learned the value of volunteering and other hobbies as a way to add a more human layer to my workplace brand. It was a natural extension of those lessons that once I became comfortable with what I do that I explored freelancing.

Freelancing is not for everyone. Some employers frown on it as a potential conflict of interest. So let me broaden my definition of freelancing to include any means you have for practicing your learned skills. Like with foreign languages, certain skills are lost if you do not practice.

If you have the time, you too may want to look into using your skills as a freelancer. This is especially doable if you are a good writer or proofreader. The lesson I learned is that, when I take stock of all the skills I have obtained from work and my hobbies, there are a lot of ways I can market myself. Why not practice those skills, practice selling yourself (for your next job), and earn some side money at the same time by freelancing?

I say this with all sincerity, particularly given the state of the economy of these days. Rather than one full-time job of 40 to 50 hours a week, many of us are finding temporary jobs, independent contracting, and self-employment. These kinds of work are only going to become more common, not less, as the nature of the social contract between employer and employee changes. Freelancing just might become a fact of life for you, me, and the rest of the country.

Now, not every freelancing gig would make a lot of sense. For example, serving as a freelance speechwriter for a politician that is working against your company's interests is more likely to backfire on you in your day job, no matter your own personal politics.

Likewise, if you try freelancing in an area or with a skill you have no expertise in, then you may end stumbling badly and hurting your self-confidence and reputation.

My main freelancing projects at the moment are my books, such as this one. I also participate in screenwriting contests. Now, as I delve into training as a field, I could easily see myself as a lecturer or even an adjunct professor at some point. Of course, I would also love to write speeches or have Hollywood buy one of my scripts.

Ultimately, though, what you choose as your freelancing gig(s) is less important than that you are trying to improve your skill set and practice marketing yourself to a wider network than just those at your current workplace. There is no telling when doing stand-up at open mike nights could send you working for Saturday Night Live.

And who wouldn't love to do that?

Lesson 38: Freedom from Debt

Whether you aspire to be a street performer or a Wall Street tycoon, sooner or later you are going to have to learn the importance of personal finance. There are plenty of books out there that cover this topic in great detail, so I will not belabor the point here, except to say the following:

I work with pensions; I have a 401(k), and a decent savings account. I was not always so lucky. I came from a background where my family was once on welfare and church handouts. Even in college, I made poor financial choices; racking up credit card debt and avoided a weekend job even though it meant not having spending money. Even then, I knew I would need to do better managing my money, but I didn't.

After college, I used graduate school to delay the inevitable repayment of my student loans, and tuition reimbursement helped get my credit cards under control. It really was not until my loans came due that I began to settle down and get serious.

As quickly as I could, I consolidated my loans into a single payment. Even at a nice 3.625% flat rate, I was staring at a total debt of $52,000 that I would be repaying at a clip of $260 per month for the next 25 years. It is a staggering sum.

I needed help. So I drew up a budget. There are plenty of resources for you to try out. My current favorites are Personal Capital (an app that tracks investments) and NetworthIQ, an online tracker you can use that functions like an Excel sheet but has the benefit of treating each month like a blog entry, so you can see your long-term progress.

In less than 9 years, my student loans have tumbled down to $28,000 and I am on track to finishing in about 5 years, a full 11 years ahead of schedule. How did I do it? Every time I got a raise, I tweaked my monthly payments to fold in a little extra money. Once I reached my savings goal, I ratcheted up the payments a little bit more. And once I began saving enough to have a budget of money to either save even more or begin investing, I periodically dumped an extra month of payments in randomly. Every little bit above $260 goes straight to principal which, like the reverse of compound interest, will slowly snowball to my benefit.

I also avoided most frivolous spending like on annual vacations or new cars or fancy furniture. As a single guy with no kids, I am fortunate to rarely get sick, so I even have banked plenty of unused leave that I could take with me whenever I should quit the company.

For a while, I considered buying a condo before realizing how much longer my commute would have to be in order to get a decent place in the D.C. area.

Of course, not everyone can save their leave or buy their home. Yet, if there is anything you can do to put your personal finances in better shape, you will be freer to make other life-altering decisions.

I, for one, have this silly hope that I will soon get called to Hollywood and can use my savings to make my screenwriting dreams come true. Until then, my day job and I are doing just fine – with my student loans in our financial crosshairs.

Lesson 39: Your Five-Year Plan

Unless you have a strong "P" tendency in your Myers-Briggs personality type, planning for the future is at least somewhat important to you. Yet, when most of us think of the future, we might be concerned with dating, marriage, kids, and retirement. We may not be thinking about our careers.

This is why the cliché interview question ("where do you see yourself in five years?") can be so dangerous and so hard to answer for many of us. I know I have always had a hard time answering it, even after I realized just how much I wanted to become a manager.

Recently, I had a mentor remind me of the importance of that question. She told me that I needed to answer it at least for myself, so I could then ask my superiors for help in achieving any goals that are part of my five-year plan.

The five-year plan is a good approach to resolving the question. In fact, it is better than merely having a vision of a future you, perhaps visiting an island getaway while using company expense accounts. Why? This is because it forces you to think not just about the long-term, but also about what could be important in the medium- and short-term time horizons. It breaks down a seemingly impossible, or at least audacious, goal into more manageable chunks.

For example, if you were new to the company and had the audacious goal of becoming a supervisor within 5 years, having a plan lets you figure out which positions will help set you up for that eventuality, and even give you clarity on some of your current shortcomings.

When I told my boss's boss what my audacious goal was for my 5-year plan, she and I outlined some of the things I could work on to get there. A move toward managing people was an obvious step. Less obvious were projects that involve other parts of the department, moving me out of my comfort zone and more into a bigger picture view of how the organization functioned. We even discussed training opportunities.

Having a five-year plan at least gives you peace of mind regarding your career path, that you have some forward movement in your day job, even if you have yet to figure out what the end goal of those five years are, because maybe you have not discover what your dream job will be.

A five year plan ensures that you retain some aspirations; that you are not just in your day job to pay the bills, but are also seeking to grow and develop as a young professional. Realizing that distinction gives you added value as an employee.

Lesson 40: Aspire to Do Better

Jack Nicklaus, the famous professional golfer, once said, "Achievement is largely the product of steadily raising one's levels of aspirations and expectation." That is, if you want to do better and expect to do better, you can will yourself into actually being better.

This is a lesson I learned not from my work, but from my political background. I had internalized this lesson even before college, but I articulated it on the DailyKos website in March 2008, during the heated Obama/Clinton primaries. I think it is a lesson with widespread applications.

Hillary and McCain are sounding awful similar these days in their efforts to take down Barack Obama. As the (much) older candidates, both are arguing for experience; Obama is instead arguing for change and ideas. At least, that's the sound bite summary of the campaign to date.

To use the experience argument in any election, you almost have to be making the case that the existing system isn't likely to be changed by you but instead you have been there long enough to understand how it works and how to get things done within that system.

And it's not that far a leap from that mentality to going to each constituent group and striking a deal: "for your support, I will try to get you this thing X". It's like trying to be hired as a real estate broker, or an interior designer - showing off what you've done to make the case you can do just as well or better in the future, without ever having to argue about whether your methods need to be changed.

This is often known as coalition-building, but it is also known as transactional politics. For a long time, the Democrats have operated this way as part of their focus on self-identity, entitlements, and special interest groups. One person called it a "put a check by each box" electoral strategy. In this strategy, one makes specific, micro-

promises to each group within your party and presto you've got victory.

You can also see it now in Republican circles with John McCain's 2008 effort. He back-tracked on immigration to satisfy the Minutemen. Support Bush tax cuts to quiet the corporate cons? Check. Support Scalia and Thomas and reverse his stand on Roe v. Wade to satisfy pro-lifers? Check. Support the Iraq War to get the support of neocons and President Bush? Check.

Inherently, transactional politics is not inspiring. It has often forced you to either concede winnable states or rely heavily on your paid media advantages. One reason why Hillary hasn't been able to beat Obama yet has been her relative lack of a ground game and the fact that Obama can outspend her.

Of course, it's more than that, and it has nothing to do with him being a Black Guy, Geraldine Ferraro's comments notwithstanding. It has everything to do with what I call aspirational politics.

I believe it is in the realm of aspiration and optimism that liberals can find their sense of patriotism. While many conservatives are content to celebrate America as it is (and prefer America as they think it was) - liberals are very often at their most patriotic when they see a future America that they like and are willing to fight for it. The Kennedy brothers tapped into that sentiment with their call for all of us "to ask not what America can do for you," Bill Clinton did so to an extent with his talk of a bridge to the twenty first century, and now Barack Obama has done so.

Of course, aspiration is not exclusive to liberals. Ronald Reagan was popular with the American people not because he cheered America for cheering's sake; they liked him because of his sunny view of where America could end up. Even Mitt Romney [in 2008] staved off political disaster temporarily by talking about an economic turnaround in Michigan.

Liberals and many voters in general like being lifted up and told there is nothing we cannot accomplish. We like it even more when the character and ideas of the messenger match the moment in history he or she finds themselves in.

Barack Obama is a post-racial, post-machine politician trying to appeal for an end to partisanship, gridlock, and lobbyist influence in Washington. Most Americans would agree those problems exist and are at the heart of why America's leadership is either not taking us anywhere, or is headed off into the wrong direction. He is the right messenger for the right time.

The trick with being aspirational, however, is you need to be a great orator with a keen sense of our place in history and how issues related in the broader context - all while trying to convince voters to look beyond the micro-policies and transactional promises being made to their specific subgroup, to look beyond that and see a wider, national need.

All 3 Senators still running for President are fine campaigners, and would probably do a solid job in office. They all would certainly have the advisers and professionals on hand to give them the true experience and knowledge needed to handle the crises that come up. What are left up to the President personally are the judgment, character, and sense of self, to do the right thing when the time comes to make a decision.

No amount of experience as a wife or as a cancer patient is going to matter in those moments. Resume lines do not matter in a crisis. A rolodex and a bunch of IOU's won't matter, either.

So what the voters should be looking at is how the Presidential candidate is conducting himself, and whether or not his policies and record reflect the character and judgment you want when that 3 A.M. call rings.

And that being the case, given the last 7 years [of the Bush Administration], I'm convinced we don't want a President who is stubborn, angry, full of themselves, and unwilling to change the system. In other words, I'm convinced we don't need transactional politics this year. We need some aspiration and inspiration to move this country forward.

The distinction I make here can apply to other issues aside from politics. Humans for the most part, like most of the species on our planet, are constantly evolving, constantly looking for ways to improve our current conditions.

The transactional attitude that you can do the minimum, like painting by numbers, is not an inherent trait of humanity. It can and very likely will lead you astray. If you see work as a means to a paycheck and nothing else, you could very well end up in a miserable job going through the motions just trying to get by. It will add to your stress, weaken your health, and ruin the quality of your life. Suffering in a job you hate and possibly passing on other opportunities means giving up on possibly finding your dream job, that one thing that is truly your life's calling.

In contrast, if you are ambitious, never settle, and constantly learn new things, seize new opportunities, and strive to build a career around your strengths, your aspirations will get noticed and you can and most likely will find everything you are looking for.

I firmly believe this. It happened to me, and it can happen to you. All you have to do is try.

CONCLUDING REMARKS

Dr. Steven D. Cohen, a communications professor I know, once described passion as "a magnetic force that pulls you toward a specific goal" whereas drive is a push toward an obligation. It is similar in spirit to my distinction between aspirations and transactions.

You can have a drive toward promotions as a way to provide more for your family. A lot of us feel that way, and it is a great and noble thing to want to do better for your loved ones. That is why becoming a manager is seen as a sign of success by so many Americans, because that promotion can lead you to bigger and better things, or so goes the perception. Yet, even more and more of us find ourselves depressed, our work lives empty and devoid of meaning. Financial and career successes are important drivers in our lives, but they are far and away not the only ones worth keeping an eye on.

Having a passion for something can feel totally different. The young guy slaving away at a laptop in a café in order to write what could be the next Oscar-winning screenplay, for example. Or the best friend who helps the young architect find the love of his life by playing "Have you met Ted?" with every girl in the bar. Or a recovering ex-introvert stepping up in front of a room full of people in order to help his coworkers do a better job.

I have always had a passion for helping people. From the time I was in first grade and wished to God that I'd become a teacher some day because I had a crush on mine, I knew it. Even when I spent three years in a row helping Spanish teachers put on a competition by being one of the guys with a walkie-talkie shuffling volunteers and contestants around, I knew it.

One of life's tragedies is losing your passion. Sometimes you intentionally bury it, convincing yourself that an easy class was your ticket to an easy career. Sometimes you forget it because life gets in the way, as you put the needs of your children first.

The leader within you thrives on that passion. Listen to him, rediscover yourself, and stand out in the crowd by following your passion.

Passion is contagious. We humans cannot help but respond to it by finding it within ourselves. A big part of being a leader is helping others to tap into that passion, that reservoir of strength and innate talent that can help guide you to your life's calling.

For a long time, I let myself believe that I was passionate about politics and the law because it was interesting and the classes were easy. For a while, I thought speechwriting would be my way in, since writing has always been a strong part of my life. Yet, for far too long and for far too many, politics is not about helping people so much as helping themselves by making a statement about what they believe in. Most of the time, politics is about the back-and-forth of ceaseless competition. It isn't for me.

When I see the glint in someone's eye when they learn something new and everything starts to click, I cannot help but smile. When I am out there creating new resources for staff to rely on and refer to when I am not around, I know I am being useful. When I get to deliver on promises made about teleworking for staff with long commutes, and I see the relief in their tired eyes, I am hopeful that I am making a positive difference in their lives.

As long as my drive for personal growth and advancement continues to allow me to pursue my passion of helping others through creativity and training, I know that I am being the leader I was meant to be.

I hope in these last 40-odd lessons that I have learned I have shown you how I found the leader within me. I hope you learn from these same lessons, find your own leadership potential, and pave the path to your own success by following your passion.

Never let go of your passion, never give up on your aspirations, and never forget to…

STAND OUT!

Acknowledgements

First and foremost, I want to thank Shaun Murphy and Chanee Yarborough, two coworkers who helped inspire me to write this book. They both have great potential, and I hope the lessons I have learned will help them find a passion that matches their innate talents.

I want to thank Molly DeWitt for all of the positivity and encouragement through the writing process, both of this book and of my more creative endeavors. Likewise, Jewelyn Sims was a positive influence and a great mentor in the finer points of leadership.

Dr. Steven Cohen, a friend of mine since our college days, always has his heart in the right place, and is doing a marvelous job inspiring hundreds of students each year to master their fears and learn the art of public speaking. His advice has been invaluable, and his book *Lessons from the Podium* is a tremendous resource.

Lastly, I want to thank Ann Poe for putting up with my ego and poor sense of comedic timing.

ABOUT THE AUTHOR

Kenneth Kerns has over a decade of experience in benefits processing, quality management and team leadership. He specializes in data analysis and employee training. A passionate speaker and trainer, he regularly conducts training seminars for the processing staff at the UMWA Health & Retirement Funds as part of his day job as a manager of quality and disability pension processing.

Ken graduated from the University of Florida in 2002, and earned a master's degree in political management from The George Washington University in 2004. The Wharton School of the University of Pennsylvania awarded him the Retirement Plans Associate (RPA) specialty designation in 2013.

His first novel was released in 2005. His latest work, a collection of short stories entitled "The Young Mike Adams," was released in November 2013. His original sitcom script "Roommate Wanted" was a screenwriting finalist in the 2013 Creative World Awards.

Ken is available for freelance writing and consultant work. He donates time and money in support of causes such as environmental activism and epilepsy research. Ken lives in northern Virginia.